DAN
vs
PHIL

POP
CORN

THE AMAZING BOOK IS NOT ON FIRE

THE WORLD OF DAN AND PHIL

DAN HOWELL AND PHIL LESTER

EBURY
PRESS

7 9 10 8 6

Ebury Press, an imprint of Ebury Publishing, 20 Vauxhall Bridge Road, London SW1V 2SA

Ebury Press is part of the Penguin Random House group of companies whose addresses can be found at global.penguinrandomhouse.com

With special thanks to: Kel Alexander, Andrea Mercado, Ashley Smith, Carolyn Love, Courtnie Bierman, Valeria Lombardo, Aleesha Gyarmati, Aline Ilushkina, Lucy Forder, Malin Forsman, Martyna Oleszkiewicz, Ida, Sophie Milton, Alexandra Armaos, blackrabbit777, Irina Tarakanova, David Keller, Rafiqah Ramil, Sian Lacourse, Alice Wang, Amy Mijovic-Couldwell, Ashley Knehans, Beth, Mary Duffy, Kiera, Koleen Sta. Ana, Krysta Bound, Kumi McKenna, Lone Pedersson, Mia ONeill, Chontae Long, Brooklyn Arrigo, Kristina Uskova/Fan art, Elise Hagen/phanga, Holly Marr/pixel Dan and Phil, Ivana Zorn and Martin O'Neill/word clouds, Mr Bingo/hair portrait, Clarissa Pabi, iStockphoto, dafont.com, myfonts.com, Page 90-97 and 100-107 © BBC, Page 198-199 © Getty Images, Page 150 © Sims, Photography (endpapers, 3, 4, 9, 14, 15, 48, 49, 50, 63, 70, 81, 89, 98, 99, 116, 117, 125, 129, 139, 143, 154 and 155) by Dave Brown at Ape.

Design: Dave Brown at Ape. apeinc.co.uk

Commissioning Editor: Sara Cywinski

First published by Ebury Press in 2015

www.eburypublishing.co.uk

A CIP catalogue record for this book is available from the British Library

ISBN 9781785031090

Printed and bound in Germany by Mohn Media GmbH

Penguin Random House is committed to a sustainable future for our business, our readers and our planet. This book is made from Forest Stewardship Council ® certified paper.

"I DEDICATE THIS TO MUM, DAD AND MARTYN (THE BEST FAMILY EVER) AND THANK YOU TO ANYONE WHO HAS EVER ENJOYED ONE OF MY VIDEOS! THIS IS FOR ALL OF YOU! (^_^)"

"I DEDICATE THIS BOOK TO MYSELF BECAUSE I WROTE IT."

"DAN, YOU CAN'T DEDICATE YOUR BOOK TO YOURSELF."

"WHY NOT? I DON'T WANT THIS TO BE LIKE A BORING AWARDS SHOW SPEECH WHERE I JUST THANK PEOPLE THAT ALREADY KNOW HOW I FEEL ABOUT THEM AND LEAVE, THAT'D BE POINTLESS."

"IT'S JUST A THING THAT YOU DO!"

"WELL MAYBE I DON'T WANT TO DO THE THING, MAYBE I'LL CREATE MY OWN NEW, BETTER THING."

"WE'RE ALREADY ARGUING AND THE BOOK HASN'T EVEN STARTED YET."

"THEY'RE GONNA START PLAYING THE AWKWARD STOP-TALKING MUSIC SOON."

"JUST DEDICATE IT TO SOMETHING AND WE CAN GET ON WITH THE BOOK."

"ALRIGHT. I DEDICATE THIS BOOK TO THE PEOPLE READING IT BECAUSE YOU PRESUMABLY EITHER BOUGHT IT OR MAYBE STOLE IT IN WHICH CASE I'M NOT DEDICATING IT TO YOU BECAUSE THAT'S BAD."

"LET'S GO!"

Hello.

Well that's five characters out of the way.

Well done.

So how should we write this?

What do you mean?

Well we're two people talking in the same book: how are we gonna do that?

DIFFERENT COLOURS?

Nah, that'd be annoying.

DIFFERENT FONT?

That's even more annoying.

Why don't we just put our initials on the left?

Okay let's try that.

D: Hi!

P: Hello!

D: I'm Dan.

P: And I am Phil.

D&P: And welcome to
The Amazing Book Is Not On Fire!

P: Wait, how did we both say that?!

D: I guess we said it at the same time? I have no idea.

P: Anyways, welcome to the book! Take off your shoes, make yourselves at home.

D: Are they reading our book or climbing inside it?

P: They can do whatever they want with it, except eat it. You can lick the vowels on this page, though, as we printed it with cola-flavoured ink!

D: That is not true: do not lick the page. Phil, behave, we've only been doing this for 20 lines.

P: I guess we should do some kind of introduction?

D: Yes that would be helpful. I think we should start by introducing ourselves for anyone who's wondering why they've spent a minute of their life reading us deciding what it is we're writing.

P: We are Dan and Phil and we make videos on the internet! Videos about ourselves and our lives and how we fit into the world.

D: And over the years, for some reason a lot of people enjoyed these things we made!

P: All these videos and shows and crazy things we've shared with our followers came together to create this huge world of Dan and Phil!

D: And that's why we made this book. You never know what might happen in the future. The internet might get deleted, a meteor could destroy the whole world, or one of us could die and it would be really sad.

P: Dan! Don't get like that already – we're only on the introduction.

D: Oops, sorry.

P: So we want to trap this giant crazy wonderful world that we've created with our audience inside an epic enchiridion. We hope that in the distant future an alien race will stumble across it and bring it back to their mothership where we will be worshipped as their new gods!

D: Well, it's not only for aliens to worship, I was thinking more general preservation of memories and stuff but okay.

P: I guess we should tell our story!

D: But where do we start? I mean a lot happened before we started making videos.

P: RIGHT AT THE BEGINNING.

I know polaroids are old but don't you just think they look cool?

DAY 1. DAN'S MUM ON DAN'S BIRTH

What day was it?
How's this for memory, I thought it must be a Tuesday and after checking I was right! (Obviously this scarred me for life, or I wouldn't remember.)

What was the weather like?
It was a clear summer night thankfully, as the ambulance took about an hour to arrive.

What time did you arrive at the hospital?
About 3am.

How long did the whole thing take?
You were born at 6:30 in the morning after days of labour. Seriously. I was in the hospital for two days before you decided to finally arrive – late as usual.

What was it like giving birth to Dan?
It was exhausting and I had to be cut up like a side of beef to get you out (you asked).

How much more painful was it than stubbing your toe?
It was infinitely more painful than stubbing a toe.

Why did you choose the name Dan?
I chose the name Dan because I like the name and didn't know any other Daniel babies so I thought it would be unusual. It turned out to be the most popular year on record for Daniel babies. Sorry.

What would you have named the baby if it was a girl?
If you were a girl we were going to call you Yazi. I had spent my pregnancy on a beach in Kenya where there was a girl named Yazi who cooked the best prawns ever, so we thought it would be a nice name! Thankfully for all concerned, especially you, you were a boy.

Was it worth it in hindsight?
Of course it was worth it – you are the apple of my eye etc. etc.

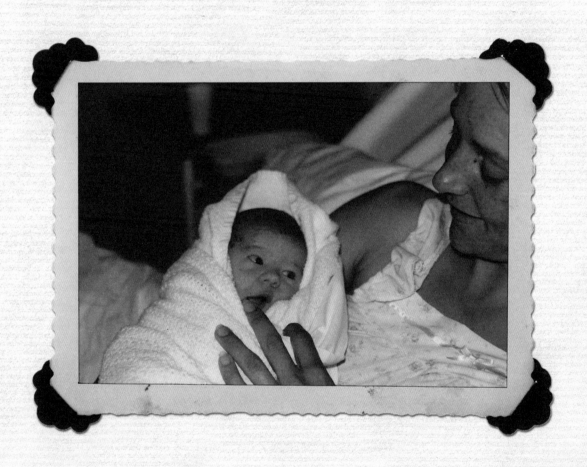

DAY 1. PHIL'S MUM ON PHIL'S BIRTH

What day of the week was it?
The early hours of Friday morning at 4am. Typical night owl Phil.

What was the weather like?
The weather was very cold, probably minus 3. Earlier in the month it was the coldest since the year 1740! There had been quite a lot of snow that month too.

What time did you arrive at the hospital?
We arrived at the hospital at about 9pm the night before. I remember the midwife reminded me of a friendly dolphin.

How long did the whole thing take?
About 8 hours! I could have flown to Florida in that time!

What was it like giving birth to Phil?
It was quite exhausting because you seemed quite comfy where you were even though you were three weeks early. I didn't have any pain relief. They gave me the gas and air machine but it was empty, aaargh!!! By the end of it I was getting a bit impatient. The midwife wanted Dad to stroke my brow and rub my back and I remember telling her I didn't want him to, I just needed to concentrate!

How much more painful was it than stubbing your toe?
It was like having 1,000 toes and stubbing them at the same time.

Why did you choose the name Phil?
I always liked the name Philip, it seemed a kind name and the Philips I knew at school were all nice people. Plus I thought it would go well with Martyn when you write Christmas cards!

What would you have named the baby if it was a girl?
If you had been a girl you would have been called Fiona.

Was it worth it in hindsight?
Was it worth it? Mmmn I think so! Hahaha, course it was: you bring us joy and happiness and I always wanted two boys so I got my wish. You were a very calm content baby and the nurses were quite surprised I had given birth. You hardly cried at all; you were very cute.

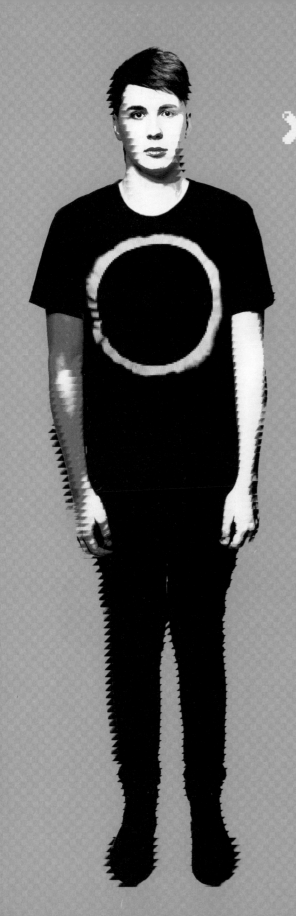

NAME
DAN HOWELL

INTERNET NAME
DANISNOTONFIRE

HEIGHT
6FT 3"

FAVOURITE COLOUR
BLACK

ANIMAL OF CHOICE
LLAMA

WEAKNESS
'SHARING SIZE'
BAGS OF CASHEW NUTS

SPECIAL POWER
PRETENDING SOMEONE'S
CALLING TO GET OUT OF
AN AWKWARD SITUATION

QUOTE
"I PROMISE I'LL DO IT
JUST AFTER I'VE FINISHED
THIS THING."

PLAYER 1 PHIL

NAME
PHILIP MICHAEL LESTER

INTERNET NAME
AMAZINGPHIL
(FORMERLY SNOWDUDE)

HEIGHT
6FT 2.9"

FAVOURITE COLOUR
BLUE

ANIMAL OF CHOICE
LION

WEAKNESS
CHEESE

SPECIAL POWER
CAN HICCUP FOR OVER
4 HOURS

QUOTE
"IF THIS PLAN INVOLVES
PANCAKES THEN I'M IN!"

A-Z OF DAN

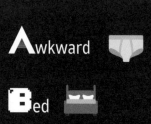

Awkward

Bed

Cool shoes

Darkness

Existential crisis

Food

Gaming

Hugs

Internet

Joking

Kanye

Llamas

More food

No

Oops

Procrastination

Questing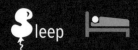

Running away from responsibility

Sleep

Tallness

Ugh

Videos

Winking inappropriately

X-files

YouTube

Zips in unconventional places

A–Z OF PHIL

Anime

Buffy

Coffee

Dvds

Eating

Final fantasy

Glasses

Hiccups

Internet

Japan

Kill Bill

Lions

Muse

Northernness

Octopi

Pokemon

Quiet during movies

Roller coasters

Superstitions

Tamagotchi

Underwater roller coasters

Video games

Wilderness

Xmas!

YouTube

Zebra

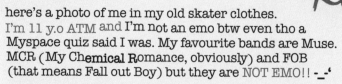

Hi I'm Dan AKA BENVOLIO Agent 003 – you know the rest.

Dunno why i'm writing this because who even would read a book that I make when i'm older xD LOLZOR JK

SKATE

here's a photo of me in my old skater clothes. I'm 11 y.o ATM and I'm not an emo btw even tho a Myspace quiz said I was. My favourite bands are Muse. MCR (My Chemical Romance, obviously) and FOB (that means Fall out Boy) but they are NOT EMO!! -_-'

Books are okay but I prefer flash cartoons on the internet atm like THE LLAMA SONG which I watch every day in the school library and can s ing by heart (Sorry i'm what you would call RANDOM It's a way of life that only cool ppl know) I got kicked out of the library once because I was playing a Hentai game on the computers LOL and ur only supposed to use them for work. I dunno why because no one even goes in the library for any reason because no one likes books JK :P

I like writing sometimes like I wrote all the things on my website (you should check it out ^^) and did a quiz once on how big a Halo fan you are so I think it will be good but I dunno what things will be in it. Heres some photos of me acting in theatre as PrinceCharming where everyone said I was awesome and another recent one of me in a hat sorry I spilled Ribena on that one

I always wanted cool emo hair (Just the hair IM NOT EMO!!) When I was older not like crazy but just cool like some pics I saw so hopefully I'll have it when I make the book when I'm older and I won't be in school anymore so thats good because I HATE SCHOOL.

I bet in the future all the chavs won't be cool anymor and all the drama and internet guys will be popular like they are on Myspace and Bebo I guess thats why I'm making a book cuz that wouldnt happen if chavs took over the world! Grr o_o

I guess I'd ask my old version if I need to pay attention in maths because it's well boring rofl.

Okay this is captain cool signing off I hope you liked my page which is obvs the best page of the book I'm gonna go buy this cool beaded necklace i saw in the shop in town hopefully I won't have rocks thrown at me for looking emo again (THERE SKINNY JEANS NOT WOMENS JEANS!! Stupid greebos) otherwise this book might not exist in the future XD bye!

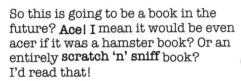

HI!! PHIL.L. HERE.
Or you can call me FLIP.
I am 12 and a half years old and live in Rawtenstall.
Or ROTTENstall, as we call it. **Haaa**.

Welcome to the best page eva ... IDST

Also I can **fly!**

So this is going to be a book in the future? **Ace!** I mean it would be even acer if it was a hamster book? Or an entirely **scratch 'n' sniff** book? I'd read that!

I wonder if smell-O-vision will exist in the year 2015. I hope so

My predictions are that I will have a rocket skateboard and maybe a beard. Hopefully I'll be a news broadcaster or weatherman with a beard and live in Tokyo or California. **I'll also have a robo** dog. Like this one **but a robot:**

I'd **ask my future self for the** lottery numbers so I could be a gigabillionaire.
I'd buy a house and fill it with tiny polystyrene balls and just throw myself down the stairs head first.

Sorry just got distracted as I spilled Fanta all over the sofa and mum is cleanin it up.

Where was I? I don't know why I'm writing this when I could be playing THEME HOSPITAL or visiting the Devil Stone with the Kool Katz

I'd tell you what the Devil Stone is but then i'd have to kill you.
NOT! Joke

Maybe by the year 2015 the KOOL KATZ will have overtaken England and you will all be members.

Who is even reading this?! Who is this **DAN IS ON FIRE** guy? What kind of name is that. Sounds like a bit of a moose.

Anyway my tea is ready so i'm gonna go. Chicken and chips. **ACE.**

Ok, I've gone! Enjoy your flying cars.

BYE

Just kidding I didn't go hahhaahahhhahahhahmaybe

Home
All About Me
Chat
Fun Fun Fun
Guestbook

DO NOT CLICK

12 Year Old Dan's Website

Dan Howell
IfYouNoticeThisnoticeThenYouWillAlsoAnoticeThatThisNoticeIsNotWorthNoticing

Hello I am **Daniel Howell AKA** Benvolio and if you came to this website to find information about me you are either insane (good for you) or horribly lost on the internet. But why don't you take your time because on this site you will find a carcrash of HTML, as well as info on me and various unrelated things. **Make sure you fill in question time and don't read theall about me bit if you're here to have fun as fun is found in funfunfun and about me isn't very fun.**
And please sign my guestbook I want to know who all my stalkers are.

This is version 6.3 of the site in which I have again nearly changed the entire website word for word.

This is the picture of me aged 12 that everyone loves but I hate so I'll show it anyway.

```
<scriptlanguage='javascript'>
//
alert ('you have successfully downloaded Trojan.exe')
</script>
```

And as most of you should know...

My Hobby's include the computer.games and.. yeah that's pretty much all I do. The two most important things in my life music, and Drama LOL DORK no but yeah. Wokingham Theatre is my claim to fame. Lol And MSM. My parents are all like 'we could cycle ten miles on a day like this go outside go see a friend!' and I would reply 'why? all my freinds are on their computers see look at my contact list if I went round we would just be on their faster more expensive computer so why not stay home?' defeated they would think 'oh well we tried'.

Music

Well as far as music goes I like pretty much everything from Bach to Dimu Borgir I love all music! except for Steps. If you look in my music collection you will find pretty a horrific mess thanks to my random downloading off limewire.

My favirote band are probably Muse seeing as Origin of Symmetry is the BEST ALBUM EVER

[INTERESTING FACT OF THE DAY] I have over 15Gb of music on my pc which is like 8 times more than anything else I have on it and when my uncle had to wipe the pc due to a horrific virus it took 2 days to finish loading up my music

Drama

(Gonna need a big breath for this) WHO WANTS TO KNOW MY LIFE STORY? no one? Inflicting time then.

Nursery - I played the lead role in my first performance ever as Santa clauses in our Christmas play and then in the Nativity I was shepherd.

Reception - The giant turnip thing I was the Farmer my first lead role check me out yeah I thought so.

Year one - Nativity again again shepherd I am gifted in the art of star spotting.

Year three –West side story modern version of romeo and Juliet I was the guy thats was Romeo I dont know his name I obviously cared loads

Year four – Cinderella The comedy I was the ponsey prince charming and I KICKED ASS like sirsly I would have gotten an academy award. Year four – Harriet the spy I was harriets best friend danny with beth as the other best friend that I was also pretty major but I can't remember any of it cuz it wus well borin like.

Year five Easter story I was the very stylish Ponchus Pilot in an Indian sauri because our poor school didn't have enough cloths.

Year five- Carousel. this was boring

Year six - snow white the comedy this was also very good I was the king but it was meh

Year eight a very busy year indeed – First the Straight talk drama club help the needy thing that went well I was an old lady and a chav it could have been better though – Second drama club Oriental fusion evening (how sad) it went well even if Ms. Payne (dribble) told us to make it less violent it was good fun Drama club three Masqerade! this was fun as I looked like a sex offender in my mask Animal Farm now this was... good in the end but we could have done so much more and seeing as the director was a stupid cow who couldn't tell her ass from her face most of the people quit because she was sooo annoying. this ended up with me being god 1, famer 1, pig 8, piano, man, piano pig, windmill and demolition expert... CLEARLY TOO TALENTED TO JUST BE THE LEAD ROLE.

Year nine the best year yet!:D:D (dork) Firstly the school drama gala was great Now... here we are, Romeo and Juliet probably the most fun I've had ever in my life EVER EVER maybe idunno I was benvolio which was a big deal for a proffesional show but it was cool Which brings me to Kes Ms.Paynes first play which was pretty good but everyone I worked with was a cock

Year 10 so far: Merchant of Venice was totally awesome!!!!1111!! we totally ka-pwned all other entries to the festivaland I won a young Shakespeare award which means I'm officially awesome

WHY PHiL was A WEIRD kiD

I'm not sure what happened to me as a child to make me so weird. My mum assures me I wasn't dropped as a baby, though my head is unusually shaped so maybe she secretly did. Another suspicion is because I spent hours every day watching an insane Japanese anime video called Robbie the Rascal. Here is the box:

My final thought is I was just born this way (sorry if Lady Gaga is now stuck in your head). You know the kittens who get millions of views on YouTube for doing really weird stuff like bouncing off walls and attacking their reflections? I think I was just the human equivalent to those kittens.

Here are just some of the reasons why I was a weird kid:

LOVE OF BRACES

I was obsessed with the idea of having braces. My best friend Jessica had them and I wanted to be just like her. I would lay in bed trying to bend my teeth forwards in the hope that one day I could have those shiny train-tracks of destiny and everyone would give me attention and want to look at my teeth.

WEIRDNESS RANKING

FISH FOOD

My grandma was impressed with my swimming skills so she told me that I was part fish (thanks grandma). I secretly ate fish food in the attempt to become FISH BOY. It didn't taste good. Don't eat fish food.

WEIRDNESS RANKING ★★★★★

METALLiC GReen ENVeLopes

As a kid I didn't want a micro-scooter, I didn't want a trampoline, the thing I wanted most in the world was ... a metallic green envelope. I have literally no idea why but I just wanted one so badly! Thankfully I've been given quite a few from my followers after mentioning it so the envelope beast within my brain has been satisfied. Thanks guys!

WEIRDNESS RANKING ★★★★★

THe SHaDow REaLM

I would frequently have long conversations with my own shadow in a world I called the SHADOW REALM. I thought this was a real place and imagined my shadow talking back to me, he was a pretty good friend actually. This all went well until I walked into the breast of a dinner lady mid shadow-conversation.

WEIRDNESS RANKING ★★★★★

TEddy BEAR DroWninG

My idea of Saturday night entertainment was sitting in front of the washing machine watching my teddy bears spin and spin and spin and spin. It's still kind of therapeutic for me to sit watching a washing machine fill with water. What is wrong with me?!

WEIRDNESS RANKING

DEMON ChiLd

I was the reason my parents didn't have any more children. Every night I would stand next to their bed in silence waiting for them to wake up. Terrifying. Sorry Mum and Dad!

WEIRDNESS RANKING ★★★★★

SHOwER BEhaviOur

Until around the age of 14 I sat down in the shower. I'm not sure if this was because I was too lazy to stand or I just genuinely thought this was the best way to shower? Give it a try one day, it's liberating.

WEIRDNESS RANKING ★★★★★

FLAT PHiL

After reading the book *Flat Stanley* as a child I really wanted to become Flat Phil. One night I pulled my entire pinboard off the wall on top of myself to achieve this flat dream. Thankfully I didn't die, but I also didn't become flat. They should put warning labels on these kids' books …

'May cause your children to attempt to flatten themselves'

WEIRDNESS RANKING ★★★★★

ThE ShoeLACe InciDent

One assembly at school I thought it would be a good idea to tie my own shoelaces together, then fall over and pretend it was someone else who did it! WHY, PHIL, WHY DID YOU DO THIS TO YOURSELF? Everyone was held back by the headmaster who demanded that no one could leave until someone admitted to the dangerous act! Obviously no one said anything and the true mystery shoelace tie-er was never exposed.

WEIRDNESS RANKING ★★★★★

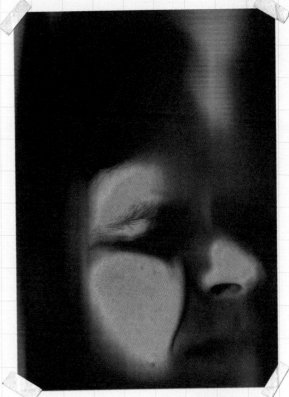

PHOTOCOPiEd FACe

Once my parents left me alone in the house for a few hours and I used my dad's photocopier to photocopy my face 100 times and then hid the pictures. I was partly imagining that my soul was being beamed into the computer system and therefore making me immortal and partly laughing at how funny the pictures turned out. For the sake of nostalgia I have photocopied my face for you here:

WEIRDNESS RANKING ★★★★★

THe WinDow

One night aged around nine or ten I stood on a chair and peed out of the window onto the roof in the middle of the night. I don't know why I did this or why I have shared this in a book that actual people will read but now you can feel less bad about the weird stuff you did.

WEIRDNESS RANKING ★★★★★★

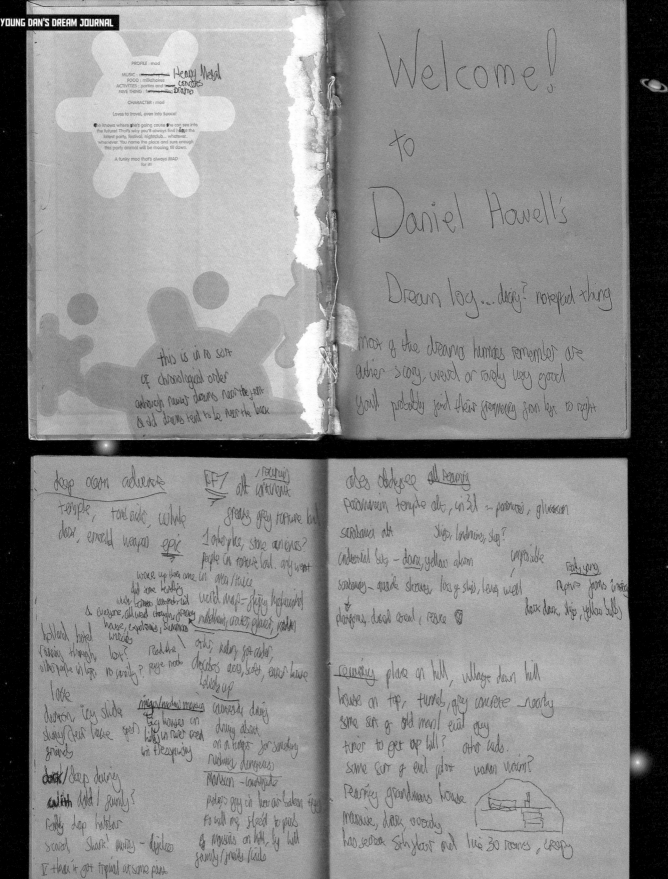

this is in no sort
of chronological order
although newer dreams near the front
& old dreams tend to be near the back

Welcome!

to

Daniel Howell's

Dream log... diary? notepad thing

most of the dreams humans remember are
either scary, weird or rarely very good.
you'll probably find their frequency from left to right

Scary dreams I remember   ages 3-16 (not chronological order)

1

I was in a dark trainstation made from Black/really dark blue tiles (like the ministry of magic) lots of people are just standing I cant see them because it is so dark - im with nana holding her hand then in an arc of tiles on the roof over the train tracks the head of like a demon comes out of the wall (much like the ancient temple boss in FFVII) looked weird of like girl but all glowing red like an alarm. it roared and I woke up.

age 3   probably fantasia related

I cant draw demons

2 "The gorilla dream"   alone or no older life   * see explanation

2 similar times - I was outside, night time, nightmare sky & music
I saw a black figure moving slightly towards me ~~xxxx~~ and on in my house - it was different to my real house it was just a room, as i remember i may have entered through the window - there was no light - only light source being the nightmare sky outside it was a plain grey plastered room with 1 table

④

I hid under the table (cheap school table ~~xxx~~) and sat hiding on. I heard it coming near. Then all of a sudden its head popped down upside down under the table and I crapped myself and woke up.

⑤ age 8   I cant draw (not physical) gorillas

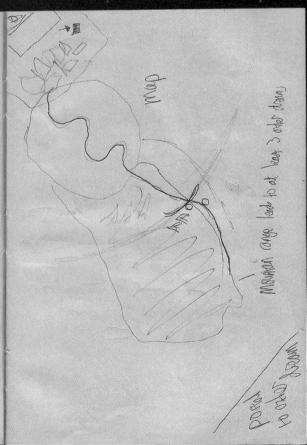

Explanation =D
Nightmare sky & music

In dreams from about 7-10 (16 in sky) in every other nightmare the sky was a brown miserably color you get green in real life also I could tell when it would be a nightmare because an eerie song sounding like synthetic strings would play (no cheesy or psycho like more slow and painful)

I cant remember how the song went exactly but I remember how the sky looks.

now that we specified this you know for future reference

~~crossed~~ **Epic dream 2**   time order wrong

military base - invading - Judy dondi?
I have a partner. Qui gon gin?
Zombies? gas mottled soldiers outside window
town pressed. have to ran away from nuke.
through rural town = epic
market tons - Jade?

links to Satan tunnel & Gw Matt

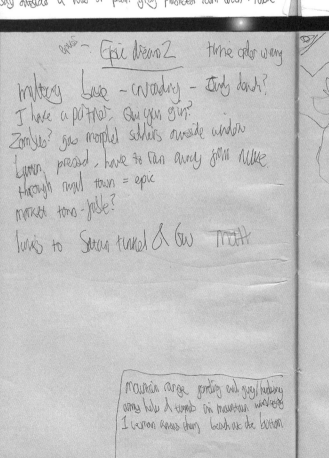

map

Mountain range leads to at least 3 other dreams

mountain range guarding evil guy/hiding army hide 4 tombs on mountain was sung I woman knows them beach at the bottom

WARNING!

UNLESS YOU ARE PHIL

THIS IS NOT FOR YOUR EYES

DO NOT READ THIS

If you read this then I hate you as you will have stolen the key.

I have included false stuff so you would never know what is true.
THIS IS ALL MADE UP.
OR IS IT?

Jan 7th

Hello! ✦ ✦ ✦
I'm going to try and write here every day
Happy new year!
our street had a huge party and I saw my brother's friend get Drunk. She got sick on my dad's coat. I don't understand his friends. Ultra Townies!!!
Today I'm going over to Anias to watch a film. Bye.
Feeling: New year.

Jan 8th
So we watched a film about an otter that got cut in half by a spade. I'm picking the film next time!
My mum still won't let me watch the nightmare on elm street but I watched some at katies ok bye

Feeling: Sad for the otter
NOoo

Feb 1st

Sorry I forgot to write. I'll do this every day. Had loads of H/W.
my friend Phil says he has a g/f but she goes to a different school. We don't believe him.
I think Kat A might ask me out as we've been talking loads on ICQ and we've had 3 phone calls. ♡
Feeling: Busy

Feb 2nd So embarrasing!!!
I was talking to Kat on the phone about an adult magazine Martyn's friend found and then
My mum picked up the phone and listened for 3 mins and said
"excuse me it's a school night and phone bills are expensive"
Do they want me to have no life? Like a cave man?
Luckily Kat found it funny but - NOT Good
Feeling: Betrayed.

Feb 18th

I hid a love letter in kat's art folder but she didn't know it was from me.
Regret it now!!
What was I thinking!!
Buffy's on now. Bye!

Feeling: STUPID ♡

Feb 22nd
~~She found~~. She found the note so I'm pretending not to know who it is from and solve the mystery what am I doing???? ?

March 18 Sorry found this again!
~~kat~~ Me and Kat went out for 2 weeks. She watched IKWYDLS on my bed but we didn't kiss or anything. We hugged.
Broke up now + better off as friends
I was sadder than her. Feeling sleepy

April 8th
I'm in Florida!
Eating loads of BBQ food and cookies.
Universal was ACE
a girl winked at me on the Jaws ride but she might have had a moskito in her eye

MAY 18
Got some rollerblades but they hurt my feet so I don't use them and dad says it's a waste of money. Not my fault. Might get a skateboard if I get money somhow. feeling: sore feet

June 4th
Our fish died.

RIP WINSTON.

feeling: Sad.

June 14 Got a new hamster Norris. He is black + white and tame. We're going to breed him with Pheobe and make babies as dad won't let me get rats or a chinchilla
Feeling: Excited.

JULY 8th GOT A SKATEBOARD?!!
Going out on it bye
feeling cool

We think Pheobe is either pregnant or really fat.
They take 17 days to give birth - longest wait ever!
Feeling: Waiting...

JULY 24 - Buffy was ace today! can't wait for the boxset

July 29 Our vet friend came over and Pheobe is pregnant!
AOL says there will be 4-12 babies

JULY 30th
Christine knocked all of my videos behind my bookshelf. What a moose.
feeling: Ultimate Betrayal

August 15th
Summer Holidays are going too fast!
Mum says boys + girls have to be seperate at sleepovers now.
I don't get why, it's not like we're all going to do it on the floor were all friends.
Might walkie talkie them

Aug 16
Kat hugged me in Swaz's kitchen as she ate dry frosties!
Swaz's mum saw it and told my mum we were kissing when we weren't!
So embarassing.
Ok bye

August 19th
I never mentioned she had the babies!
13 in total. Really cute and loads of colours.
I want to keep them all but they're going to the pet shop.

August 30th We sold the babies - £30! Loaded. School starts next week. I've done no H/W.
Might fake a broken foot to get out of football.
Feeling: Dread.

September 17th
I HATE SCHOOL

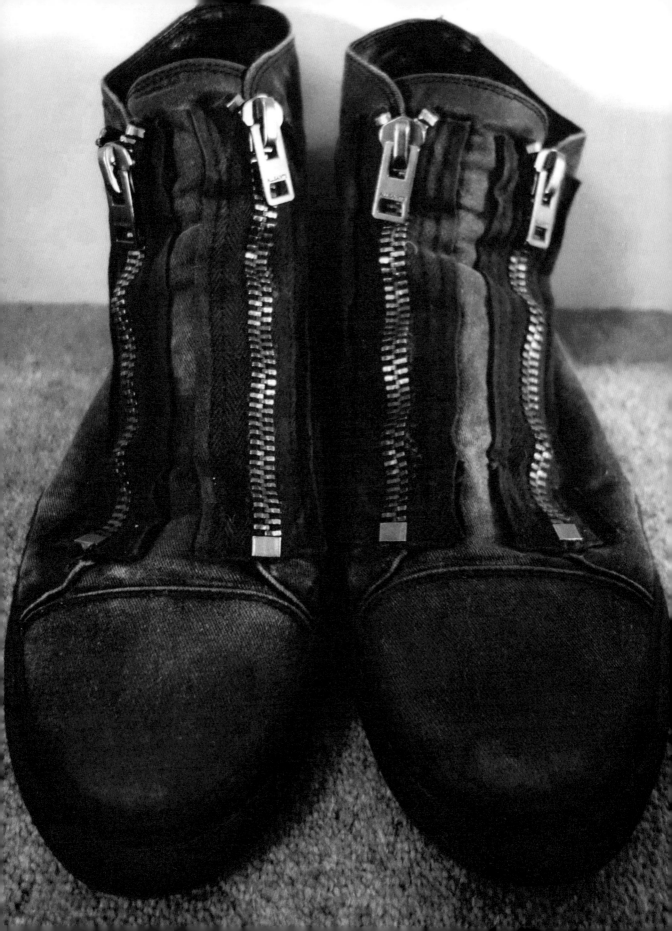

DAN'S HIGH SCHOOL LIFE

What was the first day like?

Absolutely terrifying.

The idea of going to this huge scary school filled with older, taller people - just as I had started to enjoy being the older tall person in my previous school, was perfectly represented by my oversized blazer swamping my entire body in this photo.

«««« Lol (do you see the fear in my eyes?).

My last school was so cute and tiny with only 200 ~~innocent children~~ students and the buildings were unintimidating thatched-roof bungalows. I was moving into a giant grey concrete monolith with the maths department on the fifth floor and nearly 2,000 students. I remember being herded into the assembly hall for a speech from the intimidating headmaster before we were sorted into houses. It was not like *Harry Potter*. Myself and the five kids I knew from my old school were huddled in a group in a corner trembling with fear before we were brutally torn away from each other and thrown into the swarming abyss of High School.

Maybe slightly dramatic but you get the gist.

Did you have a favourite subject?

Drama all the way. I mean how can you compete with spending 45 minutes rolling around a theatre room on office chairs? At the end, when the teacher asked for people to perform, all you had to do was say you were shy and didn't want to and boom - free period.

What was your worst subject?

'Games' - the word still strikes fear in my heart to this day. 'Games' in my school was specifically the playing of sports such as football and rugby for the allocated two hours in the timetable. I can't play football. I did tackle someone once in rugby and for a fleeting second earned words of respect from the people who usually kept whatever ball as far away from me as possible, but to be honest who wants to get muddy eyebrows at 9am on a freezing Monday morning in England?

I think the teachers actually started to give up on people at some point, as a group started to form called the 'weirdos' which was basically all the nerds and alternative kids sitting on benches listening to their iPods all year. Of course all of these people had 'reasons' such as ten-month sprained ankles, allergies to grass or 'emotional problems'. I could forge my mum's signature very well. I'm a terrible role model.

Were there any bullies?

In my school there were about ten people who weren't bullies. Being an all-boys school it was a giant wasp nest of violence and anyone who stood out was a target. I was as obnoxious then as I am now. In hindsight I understand why kids bully, they were sad themselves and insecure about who they were, so picking on someone who was a bit weird and different felt like a way to work it out. I wish someone had told me this at the time!

I could have probably drawn a lot less attention to myself by not trying to be funny and having weird hair. But in all honesty it's important to be who you are and not change for anyone; if I did then there may have never been a danisnotonfire or this very book!

Were there any embarrassing moments?

Any? Are you kidding me? Let's think of some of the bigger ones. I once was asked to kick a football back to some guys and I awkwardly booted it over a fence into a moving train. That didn't help my popularity. Oh, then there was the time I was the only kid in the whole school to turn up in full blazer and tie on non-uniform day! These are memories I've been busy repressing for years, can we move on?

Would you go back in time and do it all again?

Hahahah Hahahahahah Hahahahahahahahaha.

No.

Dan trying to camouflage himself away from bullies. It didn't work. »»»»»»»»»»»»»»»»»»»»»»

PHIL'S HIGH SCHOOL LIFE

What was the first day like?

Firstly we need a flashback to summer as I had to take an entrance exam. I think I passed and got in only because my brother told me to use the word 'flabbergasted' in the English paper. I had no idea what flabbergasted meant. Flash-forward to September! I got absolutely no sleep the night before my first day because of nerves. It was like the anti-Christmas.

I remember looking into the mirror after waking up and seeing Phil with fluorescent yellow hair staring back at me! Why had I decided to dye my hair bright yellow the week before going to a new school? Did I want to be a snowball beacon?! I have no idea.

I put on my giant new uniform and my mum made my brother and I have this incredibly «««««««««««« awkward photo.

Seriously lol at my hair. It took so much restraint not to put some intense filter over this one when putting it in the book: »»»»»»»»»»»»

We got the bus to school and I thought 'ahh at least my brother knows his way around! I'll be fine, he'll show me the ropes!' We arrived at the gate, he turned to me and said: 'I had to do this on my own so I think you should too!'

He walked off and left me. Thanks BRO. (Martyn has since apologised many times for this so I guess I'll forgive him.) Anyway, I waddled my way to class and thankfully sat next to a guy called Swaz. I told him his name was weird and we were instant best friends! Phew.

I don't remember much more about my first day other than the fact that I was very excited by Bunsen burners and the concept of homework had already ruined my life. No worries! Just seven years to go.

Did you have a favourite subject?

Probably art! It was just an excuse to talk to people whilst pretending to sketch a bowl of fruit. I remember covering my hands in black ink once to create a painting called 'THE DEATH OF DREAMS'. So deep.

What was your worst subject?

I hated P.E. with a fiery vengeance. I had zero coordination and angry northern teens on a football pitch were the worst. I forged so many sick notes! I think I had a 'broken toe' for about twelve weeks and I'd actually hobble past teachers pretending it was broken. In my final year I actually chose 'community service' instead of P.E. so I went to the house of an old lady and helped landscape her garden! Much better than rugby.

Were there any bullies?

Thankfully my school was actually pretty friendly compared to some in the area! There was one terrifying guy though, he looked like the crossbreed of a human and an actual rhino. He was so angry ALL THE TIME. My strategy was to never make eye contact, avoid him in corridors and ask to move if we ever got sat remotely near to each other. I only had one run-in with him when he pushed me over and emptied my pencil case over my head. I definitely regret not telling anyone about that thinking back as he was probably making a load of other kids miserable too. Stupid rhino boy! I hope he feels bad now.

Were there any embarrassing moments you can talk about?

I called about 17 teachers 'mum' during my time at school, including one male teacher *crawls into a burrow of shame*. Also my prom date was a balloon. »»»»»»»

Would you go back in time and do it all again?

No way! Those years felt like an entire lifetime. It's so refreshing closing that door behind you and starting a new part of your life. A lot of people are scared by the crushing responsibilities but I was just happy to never have a double maths lesson ever again! I do wish I could have kept the lion suit I wore on my last day of school though, even if it did smell mildly like a wet dog.

Name: Daniel Howell

Year: 9

Attendance

95% Seemingly misses all games lessons due to medical issues. We hope he's ok.

Academic Performance

Seems to enjoy arts classes and English but has complained about maths and French teachers? Not understanding an irish accent and claiming your teacher eats dogs biscuits is inappropriate.

General Behaviour

(Detentions - 43): Daniel is what we call a low-level disruptor. He constantly talks and this is a distraction to his friends and is affecting their learning. Several students have requested he be moved to a table in the corner where he can't be annoying.

Parental Guidance

We suggest you talk to Dan about respecting his teachers and perhaps ask him if he thinks that he talks too much. I don't think all this funny behaviour will get him anywhere productive.

Name: Philip Lester

Year: 9

Attendance

99% - Was late for a class as he was attempting to sell hamsters to other students in the playground. Apparently could not attend P.E due to a broken toe which does not seem to bother him at any other time.

Academic Performance

Strong results in creative writing and art. Less strong for physics, maths and history - it's a worry that Phil thought Henry VIII was 'probably still alive somewhere'.

General Behaviour

Detentions (1): Phil brought a laser pen to school to 'shoot his friends' which we understand does look cool but could have blinded another student.

Philip seems to spend half his lessons in another universe and it's sometimes hard to get him to focus. He is also a constant doodler which makes marking his work difficult. On one occasion a 'giant tentacle monster' was covering most of his algebra calculations.

Parental Guidance

Perhaps let Phil run around outside rather than watching fantasy television shows. We are worried about his toe as it apparently not healed for six months - consider another hospital appointment. We are concerned in many ways.

 Phil L.

PHIL'S CHAT LOGS

Ahh, remember MSN?

If you are reading this in the year 2600 it was basically an online chat program where you could talk to all your friends at once! Memories include asking total strangers to divulge 'ASL' (age, sex, location), competing to see who had the most friends added, weird custom emoticons you would hide from your parents and the strangely comforting beep when you got a new message.

GONE. DELETED. MSN IS NO MORE. R.I.P.

I feel like I owe a lot to MSN! It taught me to touch type for one. I spent every waking moment chatting to my friends to the point where I no longer had to look at the keyboard anymore. Is that a good thing?

Let's give it a test ... *closes eyes*

MY NAME IS PHIK AND MY EYES ARE CLOSED AND I'M TYRING TO TOUCH TYPE!

Okay that was pretty close!
Thankfully I can keep those memories alive, as a couple of years ago I found a hard drive containing every conversation I had ever had between the ages of 14 and 18. I made a couple of videos about this and I'm still not sure why I decided to share these with the internet, but I thought I'd preserve them by writing them down here. I changed my friends' names to save their privacy (and embarrassment).

LOL
OK BRB

 Phil: Ahoy m8

Laura: m8ey sk8y

Phil: sk8er waiter

Laura: 888888

Phil: 8 8 88 88

LAURA LOGGED OUT

 P: OMG I'm watching some tv show bout a guy who ate himself

Ash: Wat?!

Phil: LOL

Phil: 7 DAYS

Laura: NOT FUNNY THE RING WAS WORST

Phil: 7 DAYYYYYyyyysssss

Laura: I'M LOGGING OUT

Phil: Oh it's midnight

Laura: Phew

Phil: 6 DAYYSSS

LAURA LOGGED OUT

Phil: Hahah ha ... um do you have any emoticons u wana trade

Gary: er i hav a glittery thing that says lol

Phil:

Dayne: can u keep a secret plz

Phil: did u kill sum1

Dayne: noo i kissd stace

Phil: wow like kiss kiss? french kiss

Dayne: yeh tongue like actual full on

Phil: what was it like

Dayne: i think i was bad it was kinda gross

Dayne: i was jus imaginin lickin a yoghurt

Phil: ewwr haha

Dayne: if u tel any1 ill kill ur family

Phil: wat

Phil: Yr9 camp is cumin up but most of my year have morphed into townies now

Phil: so it might be like Townie camp

Jake: yeh 95% of my skool is now townie village

Phil: ppl think I'm a mosher ... but i just wear black jeans sumtimes

Jake: uh yeh i think ppl should stop with the labels ...

Jake: but i might get a tattoo when I'm 18 lol

Phil: yh i want lyke some stars on my chest or sumthin

Phil: or maybe buffy on my face lol

Mike: I found a word that rhymes with orange

Phil: No u didn't

Mike: Lozenge

Phil: That doesn't rhyme

Mike: Ur mum doesn't rhyme

Phil: I rhymed ur mum's dad

Mike: wtf

Kelly: i think i fancy Dave but i duno cz he got wiv kate

Phil: don't be a muppet. i'm sure theres some other guy you might like? somewhere like? um

Kelly: are you being nice becos ur nice or becos sum1 is being unnice behind my back?

Phil: Wat

Kelly: if u dont know i can't explain it

????: ASL?

Phil: 93/F/USA

????: shut you

???? WENT OFFLINE

Phil: I got a 3330!

Phil: a nokia! SPACE IMPACT BBY

Ash: omg let me play it tomorra

Phil: if u get me smthin from the ikki van

Ash: ok

Phil: My mum says there is a ghost in the apartment

Rachel: when you shiver it's a ghost tickling ur ass bones

Phil: I thought that was someone walkin over ur grave

Rachel: I don't hav a grave

Phil: lol

Rachel: lol

Phil: wuu2

Rachel: gota go

RACHEL WENT OFFLINE

Phil: gotta ghost

Phil: nvm

Phil: OMFFFGGGGGGGGGG99

Ian: wat

Phil: Playing darts and I threw one right in Sarah's bare foot
I FEEL SO BAD

Ian: u are a disaster with legs

Phil: omfg i got shouted at in maths

Squall: why?

Phil: I laughed at smthin in the txt book as their name was spelled wrong and it was called POODEEP

Squall: lmol

Phil: urge I'm just tryna decide on my top8

Misty: am i in it?

Phil: you are 4th

Misty: ?? jk rite?

Phil: you are in the top row

Misty: ohmygod i can't believe you hate me

Phil: go coment my new profile pic n ill put u at 3 =P

Adel: dya wanna go campin

Phil: where?!

Adel: my back garden

Phil: well new Buffy is on ... bt mayb l8r

Adel: God! u like Buffy more than ur mates ur sad!

Phil: oh i mean i could tape it but my dad needs his tapes

Phil: asl

veamp: 15/f/uk

Phil: u on myspace

veamp: yea veampoxo

Phil: gud face

veamp: thanks jus added. cool hair

Phil: thanks yeh I'm just polishin ma snowboard

veamp: kooool

Phil: hang on er norris is loose

veamp: ... wtf is norris

Phil: ma hamster he's outta his ball

veamp: went OFFLINE

Phil: bye then

Phil: LOL GUESS WHAT HAPPENED

Myles: wattt

Phil: i fell ova a bin an landed on another bin

Myles: hahahhaha wtf

Phil: sum yr11 is now calling me bin child

Myles: BIN CHILD I'm so callin u bin child

Phil: pleez don't call me bin child

BIN CHILD: lol i changed my nick to bin child

Phil: …

BINCHILD WENT OFFLINE

Phil: did u c i put a note in ur pencil case lst week

sara: ????????

sara: i lost my pencil case

Phil ::(

sara: what was the note

Phil: nvm it was just a doodle

sara: o

Phil: I h8 skool

Phil: i hid ma kit from my mum and faked a note. double escape

kyle: i told them i had a blood disease

Phil: GOOD IDEA

Phil: u don't have a blood disease rite? lol

kyle: no lol

kyle: we shd play dreamcast at mine

kyle: chippy

Phil: omg yes

Phil: mum sed i need sum fruit in my life. i told her fish is a fruit and she sed ok lol

kyle: hah lol

Phil: MY mum says I can't have more than 10 ppl at the party

Lo: but i sed kate could come

Phil: which kate i swear the whole skool is a kate

Lo: the one who sat on her hamster and cried in the pet thing

Phil: omg

Phil: ok she can come

Well that made me cringe so much I may have gained abs. Or maybe I ruptured my spleen? I'm not sure! I'm glad I kept them though, it's nice to have a little window into Phil of the past.

OVER AND OUT

I don't know why I'm writing like I'm using a walkie talkie.
I think
I had too much coffee before starting this.

Phil's YouTube Origin Story

Okay so that's enough of 'previously on Dan and Phil'. Now you have a pretty good idea of our early years in those dark times before YouTube and you're ready for the REAL story – why we started making videos.

Reply · 825 👍 👎

I owe a lot to Santa, as my first spark of creative inspiration came from the 'NINTENDO SIXTY FOURRR!' moment of me getting a hand-held camera for Christmas!

If only I still had the same style as back then

I spent entire summers making horror movies and fake TV shows with my friends. Here I am being brutally murdered and drenched in ketchup.

Fast-forward a few horrifying years of puberty and we reach the true beginnings of my YouTube channel... a cereal box. A cereal box with tokens for a free webcam. Yep, I owe my entire channel to a strangely great cereal promotion.

I made my account way back in 2006. I am a YouTube dinosaur! I was obsessed with a channel called 'LonelyGirl15' which was an American girl vlogging in her bedroom about her everyday life and her strange parents who turned out to be in a cult that sacrificed her. However (thankfully) it turned out she was an actress and none of it was real. I was mindblown and heartbroken and this is why I have trust issues.

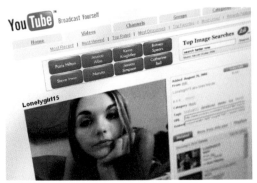

The concept of her vlogging was real though, and that's what inspired me! I loved that you could share a little bit of your life with anyone in the world by putting videos on this website. I watched more and more people like Smosh, AndrewBravener and CommunityChannel and then on 6 March 2007 my cereal webcam finally arrived and I plucked up the courage to film and upload my first video. The next morning I had an email; I had my FIRST SUBSCRIBER! I was so excited. It was a guy named 'Dudeneedaeaseonup' who, funnily enough, I later became friends with in real life!

👍 140,855 **40** 👎 328

AmazingPhil

Videos | Favorites | Playlists | Groups | Friends | Subscribers | Subscriptions

Roar　　　　　　　　　Subscribe

AmazingPhil
Style: Variety
Joined: February 07, 2006
Last Login: 2 minutes ago
Videos Watched: 15,665
Subscribers: 5,649
Channel Views: 58,297

DIRECTOR

Name: **Phil**
☆
I'm a student in York, UK.
I like lions.
I like interesting people
I play Tim in upcoming film 'Faintheart'
Check it out on IMDB!
———
Check out the people I subscribe to, they are the
reason I make videos. :]
———

☆ CONTACT ☆

Ask me a question or
send me something interesting and I might put it in a
video =D

———
☆
City: **York**
Hometown: **Manchester**
Country: **United Kingdom**
Interests and Hobbies: **Being on gameshows**
Movies and Shows: **Buffy! Neighbours LOST SKINS
Big brother HEROES Kill Bill Magnolia Requiem
for a dream Nowhere Run Lola Run**
Music: **MUSE!**
Books: **Northern Lights.. Curious incident Black
hole Life of Pi Cell by Stephen King. I think it will**

The Magic Box of Mystery
From: AmazingPhil
Views: 4,002
Comments: 313

Videos (80)　　　　　　　Subscribe to AmazingPhil's videos

Videos | Most Viewed | Most Discussed　　　　　　　　Search

The Magic Box of Mystery
03:30

Musical Socks
03:31

AmericanPhil
00:38

First video –
Phil's Video Blog, 27 March 2006

It took me over a year and 30 more (terrible) videos to get to my first milestone of 100 subscribers – that was a huge number to me. Imagine if they were all sat in my garden! Little did I know these numbers were going to grow a little bit over the next nine years. I wonder what the Phil from that first video would say if you told him?

'ACE!' probably.

Okay, it's taking all the will in the world for me to press play on this video. Here we go
hides behind a pillow.

'Ello I'm Phil.'

I was so Northern sounding! I like that I didn't bother to make any edits at all, it was just a direct upload from a black and white webcam. I didn't even introduce myself in any way I just dove straight into the topics of Mother's Day and exams. I wonder what those snake-like things all over my radiator were? It was probably my super-cool collection of skater belts. There's even a cameo from a lion! I guess I haven't changed that much.

Dan's [YouTube] Origin Story

I was a YouTube fan.

A friend from school when I was 14 once showed me this thing called his 'subscription feed' on his laptop. It was filled with videos uploaded by people with strange names like 'Paperlilies', 'Charlieissocoollike', and 'ShaneDawsonTV'. This discovery would ruin my life. All I did all day and all night from that point in my life was watch YouTube videos.

Reply · 825 👍 👎

Back before they changed how YouTube profiles looked, there used to be a stat of how many videos you had watched – mine was 39,789. That's a lot. I watched everyone's videos, I commented on them, I even spent most of my money on shirts with YouTubers' faces on them. As a daydreamer I constantly fantasised about one day being a YouTuber too. I used to spend so long thinking about it that I had the whole thing planned out in my head! What my name would be, what kind of videos I would make, even what music I'd use in the background.

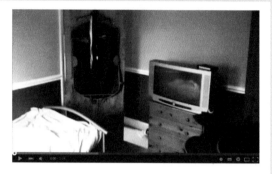

Then fast forward to Summer 2009 – I decided to take a gap year. Now what would I do with this last year of freedom before going to university to study Law? Do some early studying? Get some work experience? Travel the world? Nope. I decided I was finally gonna start making YouTube videos. I didn't tell my mum, she wouldn't have approved.

You see quite uniquely, unlike most other YouTubers at the time who started vlogging to no one about nothing in particular in 2005, I had a plan. I had years of notes, scribbled when I probably should have been paying attention to my maths teacher, of exactly what I wanted to do. I started asking for tips from everyone, including AmazingPhil who I endlessly messaged on Twitter until he followed me back, so I could harass him on Skype about things like what program I should edit videos on and where I could totally legally procure it. I got everything prepared, clicked record on my terrible laptop's webcam and set my plan in motion.

The rest is history ... or at least relevant enough for this to be a page in this particular book that happens to be about me. And that's the story of danisnotonfire!

danisnotonfire's Channel Subscribe | All | Uploads | Favorites

Search
Date Added | Most Viewed | Top Rated

PROCRASTINATION
8,410 views - 3 days ago

BUTTERFINGERS
8,906 views - 1 week ago

HELLO INTERNET.
7,112 views - 2 weeks ago

0:00 / 3:32 | HQ

Info - Comments - Favorite - Share - Playlists - Flag

PROCRASTINATION
From: danisnotonfire | October 27, 2009 | 8,410 views

874 ratings ★★★★★

this actually happened,
i suck at life. xD

NEW VIDEO ON SUNDAY!

View comments, related videos, and more ... (more info)

danisnotonfire
Subscribe
Add as Friend |
Block User |
Send Message

Subscribers (4668)

see all

Profile

Name:	Dan
Channel Views:	15,118
Style:	Variety
Joined:	October 12, 2006
Last Sign In:	9 hours ago
Videos Watched:	39,789
Subscribers:	4,668

A variety of videos including me
talking/acting and trying to be what I
percieve to be humourous.

About Me:
Heloo :]
my name's Dan.

New videos coming soon!!
So subscribe and stay tuned! :D

I make video's to keep me sane,
but don't take me too seriously.

My goal is to spread some happiness
and thought onto the toast of your day
:)

Please comment and subscribe!

Recent Activity

danisnotonfire favorited a video (10 hours ago)
51 Best Kid Fails: Barely Compilation
Kids fall and flip and fail DANCE REMIX style.
Music by: http://www.myspace.com/jakechudnow

MORE BARELY:

Subscribe!
http://www.youtube.com/subscription... more

danisnotonfire commented on CUTE HALLOWEEN CAT!! (10 hours ago)
"lmao this is the perfect example of why you're by far the funniest
person on youtube"

danisnotonfire commented on Go Act Like The Little Kid You Are
(10 hours ago)
"i liked this video :) nice message"

danisnotonfire commented on PROCRASTINATION (20 hours ago)
"lunch at 11am, know exactly what you mean. haha"

First video –
Hello Internet, 16 October 2009

DAN

0:11 / 2:34

TERRIBLE EDITING, resulting in 4 seconds of silence
between each agonising jump cut, and my general
immature behaviour that makes me want to rip my
face off when watching it. Don't make me watch
this video. I will swan dive out of the window of a
skyscraper to avoid watching this video.

1:17 / 2:34

Why is this video still public? I thought (as I still
think) a good first video would be an introduction!
Say who you are, why you're here and what you
want to make before inviting strangers to spy on
your life. Unfortunately I didn't account for my

👍 117,279 **43** 👎 245

Q&A - What was your first word?

- Why do you always make cat whiskers on your face?

- If you had to lose your leg or your nose what would you lose? ~~scribbled~~

- How do rabbits get protein?

- Ninja or Pirate - ~~scribbled~~

~~scribbled~~ I am naked right now

- Should I ever bother washing that your feet?

- Do you use an iron to ~~straighten~~ your hair?

- What does a ginger smell like

- Do you have eye lashes
- Can you say something in French?
- the rest of your life if

- Would you eat ham every day if you get paid $1 million for every month you live?

- Is your house still haunted?

- I think you should quack

- May I stroke your glasses
- Will you and your lion ever have a threesome with Hannah Montana?

- Is it weird being a man now?

- Who was your first love? ~~scribbled~~

- If you came with a worry life what would A say!

PHIL IS NOT ON FIRE

P: The video that started it all.

D: Though really, where the hell did this idea come from?

P: Well Q&As are always popular videos! We all like getting to know people we find interesting on the internet, but it's always a bit awkward reading out the questions yourself – so I thought why not ask you!

D: The Q&A bit is easy to understand but what was with the whiskers?

P: I think I must have been some kind of feline in a previous life as whenever I saw a black marker-pen on my desk I had to put it on my face! I don't think I ever actually explained it.

D: You realise more than anything we'll ever do, this is our legacy?

P: Why do you think it was so popular?

D: Are you asking who would want to watch two random guys with weird haircuts answer strange questions while rolling on the floor looking like cats?

P: The Internet?

D: The Internet. Though also I think your really quick jumpy editing made the whole thing have a strange *Alice In Wonderland* trance-like vibe.

P: Are you saying we hypnotised people?

D: Probably. Let's be honest. So how did it become a yearly tradition?

P: I think, kinda like this book, it's about respecting our origins! It's like our annual ritual of remembrance as if we're pleasing the cat gods up in the sky.

D: I was going to say because our audience loved the videos but if you're saying cat gods I won't argue with you.

P: Either way I think it's a series we should continue for the rest of time. It is the foundation of Dan and Phil.

D: It will truly be remembered among the best series of our times – *Star Wars*, *Harry Potter*, *The Lord of The Rings* and Phil is not on fire.

HAM OVERLOAD

WHY DO YOU ALWAYS MAKE CAT WHISKERS ON YOUR FACE?

IMAGINE MY FACE WITHOUT A NOSE

YOUR MUM.

VOLDEMORT IS PRETTY FIT TO BE HONEST

EVERY ANIMAL MAKES THAT NOISE WITH YOU

I AM NAKED RIGHT NOW

LET'S GO FOR IT

NINJA

EVERY ANIMAL MAKES THAT NOISE WITH YOU

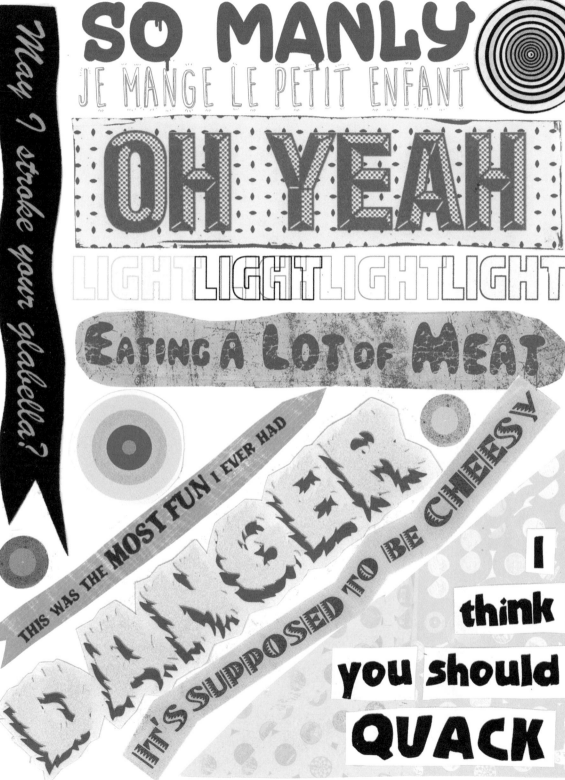

CORDLESS HAMMER DRILL

SO MANLY

JE MANGE LE PETIT ENFANT

OH YEAH

LIGHT LIGHT LIGHT LIGHT

EATING A LOT OF MEAT

May I stroke your glabella?

THIS WAS THE MOST FUN I EVER HAD

DANGER

IT'S SUPPOSED TO BE CHEESY

I think you should QUACK

HOW TO DRAW the PERFECT CAT WHISKERS

DRAWING CAT WHISKERS ON SOMEONE'S FACE IS AN ANCIENT AND POWERFUL ART FORM. YOU CANNOT SIMPLY SCRIBBLE ON SOMEONE WITH THE FIRST PEN YOU FIND, THERES A FINELY HONED METHOD WHICH WE HAVE PERFECTED THROUGH HALF A DECADE OF CAT-THEMED RITUALS. WHEN YOU ARE READY, LET US TAKE YOU ON AN ENLIGHTENING JOURNEY.

1 **Find a friend** You cannot cat-whisker yourself. I mean you can but that's kind of sad so go find someone even if it's a baby or your grandma.

2

Find a pen This can't just be any pen! Trust us when we say there are so many mistakes to make here. Do not use a permanent marker. Unless you enjoy scouring black ink out of your pores for two weeks and covering your face suspiciously with a scarf when the pizza delivery guy arrives, don't use a permanent marker – find a nice black dry-wipe.

3

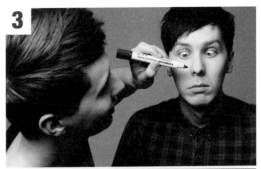

Assume the proper whisker-drawing stance It's very awkward drawing on someone's face. You will find yourself leaning around them in intimate and strange-seeming ways to properly contour the curve of their nose. Make sure you have the proper elbow room to commit to the full length of a whisker – there's nothing worse than a whisker that's clearly been drawn in two parts.

4

Touch pen to face Start with the nose. Cover the front of their nose bulb with a smooth circle of black ink. Don't scratch at it randomly or you'll do that weird thing where the pen actually rubs off bits of it that you've already drawn and then it'll go all flaky and go over your hands and it's really gross and stuff.

5

Getting started Starting about half a centimetre out from the nose, draw one smooth straight line ending parallel with the edge of the eye. Each whisker should be exactly 22.5° apart.

6

DON'T TOUCH Trust us, we know it's itchy. It will be unbearably itchy – but do not touch. You cannot ruin the hours of preparation and perspiration that will have gone into this by caving in to your physical desires and scratching your nose. If you lack the self-discipline, consider asking your companion to temporarily restrain you until you are ready.

7

And there you have it! A perfectly and professionally applied cat whisker look ready for you to answer strange questions sent by weirdos on the internet, or maybe just role-play as a cat for your own enjoyment. Method ©DanandPhil

Dan's University Life

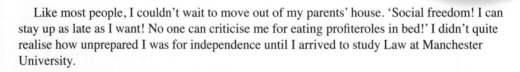

<u>**Day One**</u>

Like most people, I couldn't wait to move out of my parents' house. 'Social freedom! I can stay up as late as I want! No one can criticise me for eating profiteroles in bed!' I didn't quite realise how unprepared I was for independence until I arrived to study Law at Manchester University.

It happened in the middle of a supermarket. Myself and five complete strangers who I met an hour ago and that I was going to be living with for a year, had all shuffled in awkward silence to buy some groceries. As luck would have it every one of them, like myself, had taken a gap year! This was great, I thought. We're all the same age and we can relate to each other's life journeys – it just turned out that most of them used their year to learn some basic life skills. I had none. I just spent a lot of time watching YouTube videos (great use of your time btw never stop that).

I don't know why this hadn't occurred to me until the moment I stopped in the middle of the dairy aisle, but I realised I didn't know how to cook. Now I'm not saying I didn't know how to make a risotto or where to get a water bath to make molecular beef porridge with truffle condensation, my knowledge of cooking ended at wondering why my toast was undercooked.

I felt a sudden moment of emptiness. My spirit soared out of my body to the roof of the supermarket and I realised from above that I was all alone in a giant city without the vaguest understanding of cooking, laundry or public transport. I had that mini internal breakdown 99% of new students have so I considered hiding by the fancy cheese and crying down the phone to my grandma, but I remembered she'd probably be at her Sudoku club at that time. No consolation for me. How had I managed to never go on a bus by myself in 18 years? I'm not sure but I realised I had a lot to learn quickly.

<u>**Accommodation**</u>

The shell-shocked state that I suddenly found myself in was reflected aesthetically in my accommodation. Obviously I left my housing application form until the night before it had to be sent, so I ended up in the least requested accommodation out of ten options.

Scenic view from bedroom

It had off-cream painted exposed concrete brick walls with rusty piping that with every expansion and contraction from heat sounded like Optimus Prime falling down the stairs.

My bed had a noticeable dip in the middle where four of the ten springs holding the mattress up had somehow snapped into concernedly Tetanus-capable

52

Accommodation

points. I then made the mistake of flipping my mattress over. Take this advice: no matter where you are, a friend's house, a new apartment or a moderately priced hotel – never flip over the mattress you will sleep on. Before me was a brown stain in the perfect silhouette of a man surrounded by a yellow aura as if swamp-Jesus was climbing over a hill doused in holy light. The heating that never turned off explained the sweat patches and permanent condensation. As you can still see from my 2010 YouTube videos, a couple of album posters and some 'Dan Mail' can do wonders to transform a small space (thank you to people who sent me mail, you were literally the only source of colour in my off-cream life).

All this being said, apart from something my friends to this day refer to as the 'phantom poo' incident (which I will not write about in this book), with enough pasta and late night kebab shop visits I managed to survive and very much enjoyed my independence and socialising.

Fan mail

Social Life

I remember the 'thing' was leaving your room door open. It said 'hey my metaphorical door is also open, come talk to me let's be friends'. I spent the first week playing Halo with the curtains drawn eventually realising you have to overcome your social anxiety if you want to use the fridge. I think I lucked out in that the random assortment of people I was put with were all very cool and interesting and we all got on very well, apart from two international students which were a bit strange (no offence to every other country in the world). The first was a guy who I never spoke to in the entire year despite living in the room above me. I remember on one single occasion at about 3am after an innocent night of exploring the city of Manchester *cough*, stumbling into the kitchen to see him in tighty-whities wielding a cleaver, furiously hacking at a whole chicken.

Dan socialising after a hard day of studying

53

To this day I'm not sure if that was a strange nightmare that infiltrated my consciousness, but the most I know about him is that he lives life on the edge when it comes to appropriate clothing near sharp utensils and gas flames. The other was a girl who was very quiet, which I attributed to some kind of generic social shyness until she finally decided to let loose on the last day of the year, when what I presume was an entire lifetime of repressed emotional outburst happened over four hours. I remember her having a heart to heart with me next to a very loud speaker blasting dubstep, in which she was possibly trying to tell me she murdered someone in Japan but I like to think I misheard a lot of it ... I removed her as a friend on Facebook.

Then there was the cool guy who liked video games, Kanye West and Anime who also shared many of my interests in fashion, books and even general 2am philosophy, until one day he told everyone that he spent all of his time gaming instead of studying and then he mysteriously disappeared. I have not seen or heard from him since. Maybe I should have added him on Facebook. Or chicken-underwear guy! Come to think of it, why don't more of them keep in contact with me? Oh, probably because every time I filmed a video they just heard a guy talking to himself in his room.

Studying

I sometimes forget and even occasionally at the time forgot the reason why I was there, ah yes, the Law degree.

Now I want to be clear. For anyone like me who saw *Legally Blonde* and was inspired by the idea of sassing out a criminal with your knowledge of hair styling, or anyone who has parents brimming with pride at your academic success and desire to study the honourable field of Law – I'm not saying you shouldn't because it's absolutely horrifying, but it's absolutely horrifying. Murders are fun, yes, understanding what exactly the Queen actually does is fun, yes, but the details of 'Contract law' aren't. No offence to contracts. 'Legal language' is basically French (no offence France). It may look like it's written in your native language, but it's so strangely worded that I had to read every paragraph in my textbook about seven times to understand it. This is when I understood the profound lesson that 'you should study something you're interested in'. If you study psychology or literature, whatever you do will always, at the end of the day, be related to something you are interested in. Three months into the semester I wanted to spoon my eyes out.

Papers from hell

One of my lecturers had a voice that I am convinced vibrated at some kind of droning frequency that makes humans fall asleep. There is no other explanation. 'Seminars' I discovered was a fancy

Dan enjoying his Law course on the floor

name for sitting in a circle of ten people with your professor going round one by one realising how little studying you have done compared to the person next to you. I survived the year somewhat successfully, but it was traumatic.

Conclusion

Well as we all know, in the summer between the first and second year I had a mild mental breakdown/first existential crisis about wanting to follow my passions and being free which somehow resulted in me actually thinking that dropping out of university to become a full-time internet hobo was a good idea.

Good thing Radio 1 were interested in us and you all liked my videos or I would have been living in a cardboard box, haha!

I am a terrible role model. Go read Phil's university story – he has a Master's degree for God's sake.

Phil's University Life

The First Day

I was in the middle of Tesco holding a selection of tea towels when I burst into tears. Thankfully, it wasn't a post-traumatic tea-towel-related flashback; it was the day before I was leaving for university and my mum was helping me buy all the stuff I needed. Cutlery, bedsheets, a bin ... Was I mature enough to own my own bin?! It didn't feel like it. I was terrified. The tea towels were the straw that broke the Phil's back.

I didn't feel ready. I didn't want to leave my family in Rossendale. I didn't like change and I definitely didn't know how to look after myself. I had an awkward Tesco mum-hug, with Janet the checkout lady watching us, pulled myself together and put the tea towels in my basket. There was no going back now, I was going. It was happening. Thankfully, it was one of the best decisions I ever made!

The car journey to York University was the most terrified I had ever been. So many thoughts were melting my brain. Will people like me? How will I know what to do? What if they are all lizard people? What if I get lost and set the kitchen on fire and what what what what?

After an endless two-hour drive, I arrived on campus with my parents and they helped me unpack my computer, pinboard, cry-inducing tea towels and, most importantly, my *Buffy The Vampire Slayer* box set. My parents offered to stay and take me to dinner but I knew that I had to rip the plaster off and be brave. I walked them to the car, waved my goodbyes and returned to my room.

I was alone.

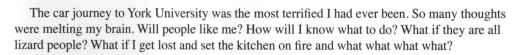

Accommodation

York University is beautiful! A huge flowing campus of lakes, geese, statues and old-fashioned houses. (Small fact: If you kill a goose then you are banned for life, but if you kill a person you can return to campus after you've finished your sentence! They do love their geese.)

Unfortunately my accommodation was not beautiful. I was in a house of five girls, five boys, two toilets and one shower. ONE SHOWER? What were they thinking?! My stomach sank when I realised I'd have to share a bathroom with other people. To make it worse the toilet was right next to the kitchen so there was no privacy at all! No more hour-long phone sessions on the toilet.

The walls and ceilings were about as thick as a sheet of cellophane. I could hear EVERYTHING. I could even hear the guy in the room next to mine peeing in his sink *shudder*.

I've repressed most of the other things that I heard. I bought some bomb-disposal-strength ear-plugs so that kinda helped.

A guy I met on the way into my bedroom told me they always put a tall boy in the room next to the front door as he'll be able to defend himself from burglars a lot easier. THANKS PETE. Thankfully, my door had three locks on it and I had an elaborate escape plan involving my window and an imaginary training montage of ninja skills.

Besides the lack of toilet, strange stains and high probability of burglar death, I had actually made my room pretty homely. Comfy duvet, laptop, DVDs, sink, what more could I need? Food. Not even a single raisin in my room. It was time to venture into the kitchen.

Social Life

When it was time to meet people, my brother's advice was buzzing in my mind:

Brother advice 1:
'Maybe don't reveal all your quirks and your Buffy obsession straight away.' BAD ADVICE. People definitely click less with you if you hold back your personality! It turned out my university housemates were way more relaxed and actually embraced any weirdness in the house.

Brother advice 2:
'Prop your door open with an open box of Haribo.' GOOD ADVICE.
My bedroom was next to the front door so I met loads of other students as they were moving in too!

I hung out in the kitchen for the next few hours and made an effort to introduce myself to every person who entered even if they didn't immediately seem like they were Phil compatible. It was a really diverse mix of people: sporty girl, art students, a guy into heavy metal, a guy who wore fluorescent green shorts every day and even a girl from North Carolina! I struck up a conversation with a guy called Andy from New Zealand and we bonded over the TV show *LOST*. I think I may have weirded him out slightly by immediately suggesting we go watch it on his bed. My social skills needed a bit of work, okay?

First day of uni with my new housemates!

The plan for that first night was to go out to a club AKA my worst nightmare. I hadn't planned for this. I can't dance! What was I gonna do? It didn't turn out to be so bad. I just kinda bobbed my head up and down like a chicken on the dancefloor and jumped around to The Killers for a few hours and got to know my new housemates a little bit.

Of course living with ten people is never going to be easy. I bonded with one girl over Crash Bandicoot until it turned out she didn't like Crash Bandicoot and was only playing it as she thought I fancied her. When I said I didn't see her that way and that I was only in it for the Bandicoot, she threw a drink in my face. Who'd have known Crash Bandicoot could be so dramatic?

The guys of the house also began a prank war against each other. Their first attack on me was one of the most severe. I got back from a lecture and my whole bedroom was empty apart from a note reading 'Go into the kitchen'. I walked into the kitchen to see they had moved my ENTIRE bedroom into there. Even my computer was set up and switched on on the kitchen worktop! Of course they didn't help me put any of it back. Lesson to learn from that one: LOCK YOUR DOOR.

I wasn't much of a prankster so I never really got revenge. Oh wait, I did put salt in their sugar once. Somebody stop me.

I got the entire house to bond one weekend by making Andy wear a tinfoil mask and filming a horror movie set in the future for my channel called 'THE GAME'. It was actually my first video upload to AmazingPhil before I started vlogging!

Another thing that went down in history was the moment I forgot I was making toast at the exact time the toaster decided to break and stay switched on, melting the entire toaster, filling the house with smoke and calling out the fire brigade.
Oops.

Throughout my uni years I went from knowing no one to making loads of friends on my course, bonding with my housemates and even moving in with 5 of them into our very own house (complete with mouse and creepy landlord who occasionally slept in our garden in a tent)! I'd like to say I keep in touch with all of them now but unfortunately life isn't like that. Friends change and drift apart but I'm sure we'll cross paths again someday.

Studying

Oops I never actually said what I was doing at university. That's kinda the whole point you are there right? I was studying English Language and Linguistics after loving English Language at school and having a genuine interest in languages. I'll be honest that 50 per cent of my degree was a confusing waffle-fest of 3-hour lectures and near-impossible homework. The exams were hard too. Rocket science hard. I think I chewed through so many pens in one exam that the biro police were launching a serial killer inquiry. I actually scraped through my first year and somehow a light switched on in my brain and I did pretty well in years 2 and 3! I stayed on to do an MA in Post-Production and Visual Effects which really helped out my YouTube and is the reason why I know how to animate Kristen Stewart's face onto the body of a small badger. Totally worth a student loan. Here's a picture of me studying hard: >>>

Conclusion

If I could go back and do uni again I think I'd try and meet even more people! I signed up to about 17 clubs and never went to any of them. Maybe I could have been super buff and in the naked rowing calendar if I'd actually turned up to the first 8am practice. Who knows?

Overall I think university was my transformation from an extremely shy caterpillar with spiky hair into a mildly awkward moth with emo hair. I'm not the fully formed flaming hawk that I want to be yet but I'm getting there? Kinda!

The University of Manchester

www.manchester.ac.uk

24 October 2012

Private & Confidential
Mr Daniel Howell

Manchester

Dear Mr Howell

I am writing to acknowledge that you have withdrawn from your LLB Law degree with effect from 06th June 2011.

On behalf of the School of Law, may I take this opportunity to wish you well for the future.

Yours sincerely

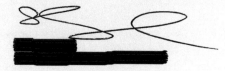

cc: Student Services Centre (Fees Section)
Student File
Academic Adviser

The University of Manchester,

HAVE MY BABIES

HAVE MY BABIES

SATAN BIEBER

BIEBER
SATAN

i am

Irish wristwatch

British

and i PHIL STRIKER

walk on

i am British and i walk on the pavement

the pavement

PHIL STRIKER

DINOSAURS

I WOULD EAT MY OWN FEET

What is with the cat whiskers?

What is with the cat whiskers?

What is with the cat whiskers?

SIDEWALK

CRACKLE

R <	O :	B *
RUN	POKE	BORDER
O ,	T >	S
POKE	RAND	SAVE (NOT)

HAVE A MASSIVE PANCAKE

HAVE MY BABIES

mega bailey's sherbet chocolate truffle candy mountain explosion

NICK

JONAS

PERSONAL

THIS IS

DON'T

DON'T THIS IS PERSONAL

CHILDREN

A wheel for a foot

ZEBRAAAAHHHHAHHHHH

SATAN BIEBER

MICROWAVE

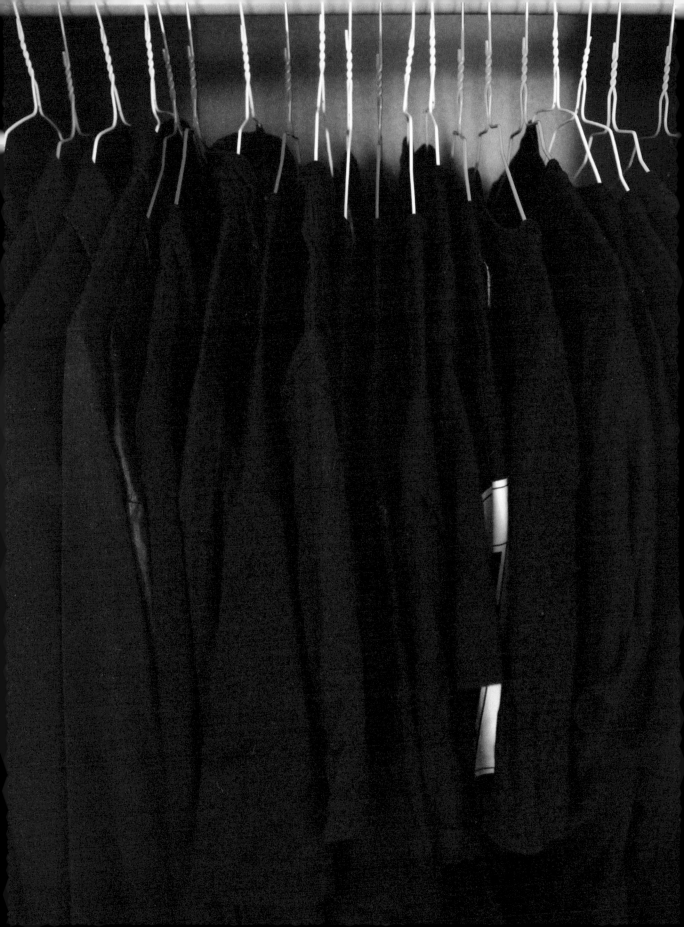

THE MANCHESTER APARTMENT

D: Ah, the first Dan and Phil pad.

P: AKA the Phlat.

D: Or the Phalace of dreams.

P: We didn't call it that and, Dan, that sounds really wrong.

D: Oh it totally does you're right, I'm so sorry.

P: Yep in 2011 after Dan gave up on his *Legally Blonde* dreams we decided to move in together!

D: It seemed like such a perfect idea. I desperately needed a place to live, Phil was going crazy living alone and we were both YouTubers!
No more feeling judged for talking to ourselves in our bedrooms at 4am.

P: Wait, what do you mean 'seemed like'?

D: So that apartment was pretty cool. I mean, it was on the 18th floor looking over all of Manchester like Pride Rock. How did we get it?

P: Total luck. I look at apartments on property websites for fun 'cause I'm a cool guy like that and I noticed this one for a weirdly low price.

D: Someone probably died on the breakfast bar.

P: It was suspiciously clean!

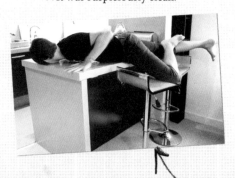

D: Although didn't we have to get your dad to speak to the owners because they didn't understand what YouTube was and how that could pay rent?

P: Yeah it turns out saying 'we make videos in our bedrooms' doesn't sound great!

D: I was just happy to escape the hell of my university accommodation. I kinda miss Manchester though, it's such a cool city with everything you'd want! I feel like I've 'done it' now though. I mean when your favourite milkshake place names a drink after you it's time to leave.

P: At least I still get to go up North to see my homeland! Do you miss the creepy guy dressed as a statue who gave out lollipops?

D: He haunts my nightmares to this day. Let's have a tour of the apartment!

BALCONY

D: This is the balcony where Phil once dropped a bouncy ball off the edge and it bounced higher than a lamppost and nearly killed a pigeon.

P: It was for science! I mainly went out on the balcony to look through the windows of the business hotel that was opposite us.

D: I'm moderately certain that's illegal.

BREAKFAST BAR

P: Didn't you once sensually rub yourself all over this?

D: Yes I think we have a picture! (opposite) The surface was just asking for it tbh.

P: Though how often did we actually have breakfast on it?

D: Not once in an entire year. It was mainly used as a thing to balance cameras on when we filmed cooking videos and sketches.

COFFEE TABLE

P: Did you know this is actually coffee table #2? Yep the first one got completely destroyed when Dan fell on it.

D: A bit of context here. I have a thing called 'orthostatic hypotension' which is the fancy term for 'really slow blood' so being an obnoxiously tall person, whenever I stand up really quickly when the blood is all still in my feet I fall over like a logged tree!

P: I kinda thought you died but then when I noticed you hadn't it was kinda funny.

D: Thanks.

BATHROOM

P: Pretty swank bathrooms actually.

D: Coming from my shared University bathrooms you have no idea how much this meant to me.

P: Wasn't this the bath where you exploded Coke and Mentos up your shirt for a dare?

D: Ah yes. I remember peeling the minty bits of shell that had fused to my flesh for weeks afterwards. Good times.

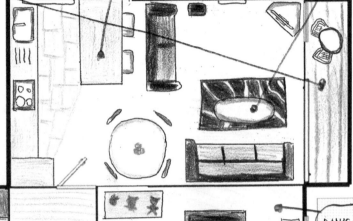

DAN'S ROOM

D: I remember the width between my bed and the opposite wall being just wide enough to sidestep through on tiptoes.

P: You made the most of what space you had!

D: I like to think that the spiritual energy of all the videos I filmed on that bed will linger in the property for years to come.

P: The spiritual energy of you ranting about people at cinemas and fanfiction?

D: I also removed most of the paint from the walls by blutacking posters everywhere but shhh don't tell anyone.

PORTAL TO ANOTHER DIMENSION

P: Little did our viewers know at the time but hidden in this cupboard was actually an interdimensional vortex!

D: This is where we hid all our alter-egos from our videos and the things that we couldn't be bothered to tidy like mystery wires and those bits of lint that just appear on the floor.

P: It was quite convenient! The forces only demanded a blood sacrifice once a week and sometimes we got to travel to the other side.

D: Remember that time we visited Other-Manchester and rode meat scooters down the hill towards the teeth shrine?

FRONT DOOR

P: This was the scene of many incidents such as 'The Holy Mother'.

D: Was that when a lady tried to get you to join a cult?

P: Yes I was absolutely terrified!

D: I would have gone along just to meet her. I'm imagining something with tentacles but I think I'd be disappointed.

P: Also once when we were taking in our shopping a drunk guy just walked into our lounge thinking it was his apartment.

D: You were convinced that we were going to die - I still remember your manly squeal. I was just happy to interact with another human.

PHIL'S ROOM

D: Wait, why did you get the bigger room again?

P: Because I had more subscribers.

D: Fair enough. I was jelly of the en-suite.

P: There's nothing like being able to sit on the toilet with the door open.

D: Dude, your bedroom door didn't have a lock. I could have just walked in.

P: Oops. ALWAYS KNOCK.

Roommate Assessment form

Evaluator: Dan Howell

Roommate name: Phil Lester

Time had as roommate: 3 years

General Tidiness:

Phil is an incredibly messy person. I don't think he's ever made a coffee without somehow spilling enough sugar and instant powder to turn the kitchen counter into an ice rink of caramelised brown goo. He leaves paper all over the office, he leaves his clothes on the bathroom floor, he leaves socks in the most random places you could imagine and worst of all – the contact lens pot. Every day Phil takes out his contact lenses, puts them in the little plastic pot and then balances them directly on top of the tap. Moving things off a tap may not sound that bad! Every. Single. Day. Is this the right section to bring up the time he stuck holographic Spice Girls stickers all over our furniture?

Household Chores:

Phil's actually pretty good at the chores! I think he stacks the dishwasher and does the laundry for fun or probably out of some kind of procrastination-related guilt, but either way he gets the jobs done.

Noise:

He will blare video game soundtracks at a dangerously high volume when cleaning the kitchen and his Celine Dion renditions in the shower aren't the best thing early in the morning, but most of the noise in our apartment we make together! That came out wrong. I meant playing video games – VIDEO GAMES.

Food:

Oh. My. God. Phil has what we refer to as a 'secret eating' problem. He'll tell me we're all about the health now and buy us salads for lunch, then volunteer to cook tofu and air stir-fries and there I am thinking it's out of the goodness of his heart! No. Roughly every 25 minutes Phil will sneak into the kitchen with levels of stealth that I'm sure would impress most intelligence services and eat something without anyone finding out. What happened to my cereal? I thought we had four cookies left not one? Where are those sweets I bought for our friends coming over later? The guilt is always plain to see within his eyes. At least he regularly buys snacks! Plus when he's not eating the food he's pretty good at cooking, so that's alright.

Bathroom Usage:

What is this thing you call a 'towel'? I wouldn't know as, despite owning five, I've never seen them as they're all on Phil's bedroom floor. Why does someone need three towels after having a shower?! Like I get two towels if you want to put one on your hair (not that Phil's really requires it) but what is the third one for? Shoulder drying? Ankle drip protection? General emotional support?? There's nothing worse than washing your hands and having to walk through the house dripping water on to your socks desperately searching for an appropriate place to wipe them.

Overall Rating: 4/5

☐ **Outstanding**   ☐ **Exceeds Expectations**   ☒ **Meets Expectations**   ☐ **Improvement Needed**

Comments A couple of issues but I guess he could be a cannibal or a beekeeper or something so it works out pretty well.

Roommate Assessment form

Evaluator: Phil Lester

Roommate name: Dan Howell

Time had as roommate: 3 years

General Tidiness:

Beware of Dan if he loses something! Generally he is quite a tidy guy but if he loses a precious sock or strange zippy jumper he will turn into a rampaging beast and turn the entire house upside down looking for it. One time I caught him emptying our box of Christmas decorations onto the floor looking for a USB cable. I mean I had left it in there, but that is not the point!

He also throws any piece of paper he finds in the bin so protect important documents with your life. Examples have included our holiday boarding passes, important receipts and my script the night before The Brit Awards!

Household Chores:

Dan's pretty great at tidying the lounge and re-arranging all the DVDs into alphabetical order. However, he still needs training in the art of not putting red socks in with white washing as I now have a lovely collection of pink shirts and boxer shorts.

Noise:

I think we are both as bad as each other when it comes to noise so I feel more sorry for the people sharing our walls! Dan usually goes to bed later than me so I occasionally wake up to him aggressively shouting at the TV playing Mario Kart.

Food:

Dan claims I'm a secret eater but most of the time I'm just inspecting the cereal to check it is still in the box and it's fresh enough for the next morning. You believe me, right? Right? OKAY I HAVE A PROBLEM but I think Dan needs to hide his snacks better, or perhaps invest in some kind of cereal padlock. It's all his fault really! If he bought some kind of cheese-related cereal then there wouldn't be a problem. On a more positive note, Dan does cook great Indian food and understands the perfect science of cooking microwave popcorn without leaving too many kernels. Side note: HE EATS THE KERNELS! What's that about?!

Bathroom Usage:

I don't know how many times Dan washes his body but don't let him loose on your shower gel as he can use half a bottle in one go. He'll also occasionally lock himself in the bathroom to practise his rendition of 'Bring Me To Life' by Evanescence (singing both the male and female parts).
It's actually quite melodic so I don't mind too much.

Overall Rating: 4/5

☐ **Outstanding**   ☐ **Exceeds Expectations**   ☒ **Meets Expectations**   ☐ **Improvement Needed**

Comments Generally a good housemate. I probably would have given him 5 if I wasn't searching for my birth certificate in a bin bag whilst wearing pink boxers right now.

Do you guys have a cat whiskers fetish or something?

I would lose the sense of DANCE

IS THIS REAL LIFE

THEY GOT SAD AND EXPLODED

Forehead birthing area

What would you NOT do For £1,000

Blow on my nose. No that's weird don't do that.

Bacteria

YOU'RE GLITTERING

⑤ ④ ③ ② ①

EAT A DOG

Hyper Kirby Plumber and Sword!

How much wood could a wood chuck chuck
if a wood chuck could chuck NORRIS

BRO

JESSICA'S PAGE

HEYA MY NAME'S JESSICA AND WELCOME TO MY TOTALLY AWESOMEFAB PAGE!!

I'M GUESSING YOU'LL WANT TO KNOW ALL ABOUT ME SO HERE'S A LITTLE THING I WROTE FOR ALL THE PEOPLE I MEET (BECAUSE I'M POPULAR):

- ♥ MY FAVOURITE COLOUR IS PINK.

- ♥ MY FAVOURITE ARTIST IS DEMI LOVATO - SELENA CAN GET OUT SHE'S SO BASIC I MIGHT MESSAGE SOMETHING AT HER ON MY PHONE LATER.

- ♥ MY BEST FRIEND IS BECKY BUT YOU DON'T NEED TO KNOW ABOUT HER SHE'S KINDA BORING LOL.

♥ MY FAVOURITE OUTFIT IS MY PURPLE CARDIGAN I WEAR IT EVERYWHERE I GO BECAUSE IT'S AWESOME FOR MY FIGURE AND SHOWS JUST THE RITE AMOUNT OF CLEAVAGE! HEHE (IT USED TO BE BECKY'S BUT I SWAPPED IT FOR AN OLD GREY ONE OF MINE BECUS I LOOK BETTER IN IT).

MY HOBBIES INCLUDE PARTYING AND DATING AND SHOPPING. SOME PEOPLE CALL ME LOUD BUT I CAN'T HELP BEING SUPER CONFIDENT IN HOW BEAUTIFUL I AM, IT'S JUST HOW I WAS BORN (DON'T BE JEL!). I'M LIVING WITH MY PARENTS ATM, AS MY DUMB EX TROY MADE ME MOVE OUT OF HIS HOUSE AFTER DUMPING ME. I MEAN WHO DOES THAT?? HE WAS SUCH A JERK. WHO CALLS SOMEONE A STALKER JUST FOR GOING TO THEIR HOUSE AND CLIMBING INTO THEIR BEDROOM AFTER NOT REPLYING TO A TEXT FOR 15 MINUTES? HOW WAS I SUPPOSED TO KNOW HE WASN'T DEAD?

MY MUM IS LIKE SUPER RELIGIOUS AND ONCE SHE TOLD ME THAT IF I DON'T FOCUS ON SCHOOL AND 'CHANGE MY PRIORITIES' THAT SHE'LL SEND ME TO A NUN PLACE. I MEAN WTF!! UGH OMG I HATE MY MUM SHE'S SO ANNOYING. CAN YOU IMAGINE ME IN THAT STUPID BLACK OUTFIT WITH A THING OVER MY HEAD COVERING MY HAIR?? THAT'D BE SO STUPID LOL.

DAN?
OH THAT GUY.
IDK HE'S WEIRD HE'S ALWAYS IN SOME AWKWARD SITUATION WHEN I'M TRYING TO PARTY AND TBH I JUST DON'T CARE.

BECKY'S PAGE

Hi um. My name is um, Becky.

People don't usually ask stuff about me so I'm not sure what to say.

I like music. My mum who's called Becky too was a big fan of
The Beatles. I mainly focus on my work. I don't think I'd really have
time for a boyfriend, not that anyone's really paid attention to me before.
My favourite item of clothing is a grey sweater,
I like it because it helps me blend in I guess.
I don't like drawing too much attention to myself.

I'm kind of shy but my best friend Jessica is really great because
she's cool and popular and lets me hang out with her. I'm grateful
for that.

What do I think of Dan?
He seems like a nice guy, I've never really spoken to him myself.
I remember Jessica talking about him a couple of times but I don't know
how much she likes him.

THE TALE OF BECKY AND JESSICA

This is a true adventure through friendship and drama. Much more interesting than Dan and Phil to be honest. **This is their story:**

Jessica encounters a pervert on the tube

06/09/2012

'OH MY GOD BECKY I JUST SAW THE TALLEST LESBIAN EVER'

Jessica gets dumped by Troy

23/11/2012

'I CAN'T BELIEVE TROY WOULD DO THAT TO ME'

Jessica tries to give up chocolate on New Year's Day

04/01/2013

'I'VE BEEN GOING COLD TURKEY FROM CHOCOLATE FOR TEN HOURS AND I'M STILL NOT BEYONCÉ'

Jessica tries to hit on Dan and friend and insults Becky

28/2/2013

'SHUT UP BECKY NO ONE'S TALKING TO YOU'

Jessica complains about Becky betraying her

12/5/2013

'I CAN'T BELIEVE THAT AFTER EVERYTHING WE'VE BEEN THROUGH YOU WOULD JUST THROW AWAY OUR FRIENDSHIP'

Jessica is at a party and sees Dan drop a pile of discs

29/10/2013

'THIS PARTY IS OVER'

Jessica confronts Becky on the phone

9/12/2013

'BECKY WHY DID YOU UNFRIEND ME ON FACEBOOK?'

INTERVIEW WITH JESSICA

Interviewer:
Jessica, when was the last time you spoke to Becky?

Jessica:
I haven't spoken to Becky in over a year... I remember she deleted me on Facebook and she wouldn't even tell me why. What a freak.

Interviewer:
Do you think it may be to do with how you treated her?

Jessica:
What do you mean 'how I treated her'? We were like totally best friends! I took her to parties, I told her all my gossip, we even swapped her lame clothes.

Interviewer:
Do you think the way you talked to her was okay?

Jessica:
Uh, what do you mean?

Interviewer:
Well, I mean from what we've seen, it seems like you talked down to her a lot and almost used her just to boost your own confidence.

Jessica:
Pfft, Becky didn't take any of those things seriously! Right? I mean, I was kind of joking.

Interviewer:
Well what do you think? Do you understand why Becky chose to do what she did?

Jessica:
I feel like this is the first time I've ever thought about it. Becky's always been there for me you know? Even our mums were friends back when they used to meet up and write weird fan fiction together. I guess I've been kind of a bitch. Oh my god I need to tell her I'm sorry.

Interviewer:
Do you think if you apologise your friendship can continue?

Jessica:
I've felt so lost without her. It was the worst year of my life not having a best friend and if I have to change to get that back, I'm gonna do it! Becky, I promise I will be better for you, just let me say how I feel.

Becky declined to comment on the situation when told about Jessica's plans to apologise.

We can only wait and hope this new found insight can bring them back together. #BESSICA4EVER

HELLO

PHIL'S LION HERE!

HERE'S A FRIENDLY REMINDER TO TRY AND ENJOY LIFE. I KNOW YOU'RE THINKING
'WHAT DO YOU KNOW?!
YOU'RE JUST A SMALL STUFFED LION!' WELL TRUST ME. I HAVE SEEN A LOT.
DON'T GET ME STARTED ON THE GREAT ZEBRA WAR AS THIS ISN'T ABOUT ME. IT'S ABOUT YOU.
PLEASE TREASURE EVERY MOMENT OF YOUR EXISTENCE AS ONE DAY YOU COULD BE LEFT TOO CLOSE TO A HAIR STRAIGHTENER AND SET ON FIRE.
I'M SPEAKING FROM EXPERIENCE. PHIL REALLY NEEDS TO STOP LEAVING THOSE THINGS NEXT TO MY TAIL. SERIOUSLY THOUGH, IF YOU'RE NOT CAREFUL LIFE COULD
PASS YOU BY AND BEFORE YOU KNOW IT YOU'LL HAVE TEENAGE CUBS AND YOU'LL BE PLANNING A NICE AREA OF THE SERENGETI TO RETIRE TO.
SAY YES TO MORE THINGS! IF THERE'S A TRIP TO THE WATERING HOLE, GO TO IT! IF THERE'S A WARTHOG PARTY BUT YOU DON'T KNOW MANY ANIMALS, SAY YES ANYWAY!
WHAT'S THE WORST THAT COULD HAPPEN? YOU'D HAVE A SLIGHTLY AWKWARD FIVE MINUTES AVOIDING HYENAS BEFORE YOU GET CHATTING TO SOMEONE?
I MET MY WIFE IN CIRCUMSTANCES LIKE THIS. I COULD HAVE JUST RELAXED ON PHIL'S BEDSIDE TABLE MINDING MY OWN BUSINESS BUT I THOUGHT TO MYSELF:
'SELF! IT'S TIME TO SEE WHAT IS BEYOND THIS BEDSIDE TABLE!'
I VENTURED AS FAR AS THE SOCK DRAWER AND MET MY BEAUTIFUL AND SLIGHTLY UNUSUAL WIFE. LOOK AT ME NOW! I'M A FAMILY LION. I'M NOT SAYING YOU SHOULD MOVE TO AFRICA
AND GET MARRIED, FEEL FREE TO BE SINGLE AND ENJOY YOUR OWN COMPANY. IT'S YOUR LIFE. DON'T FEEL PRESSURED TO HAVE CUBS AND SETTLE DOWN IF YOU DON'T WANT TO!
JUST MAKE SURE YOU REMEMBER THAT A BILLION COINCIDENCES HAD TO OCCUR FOR YOU TO EXIST AND EACH PASSING MOMENT IS A POSSIBILITY FOR A NEW ADVENTURE.

BETWEEN YOU AND ME, I KNOW THAT I'M A STUFFED ANIMAL AND I WILL NEVER SEE AFRICA IN REAL LIFE, BUT JUST SEEING THE JOY ON MY FAMILY'S FACE WHEN I BRING HOME
A SMALL PIECE OF CEREAL OR AN ABANDONED CRISP FROM PHIL'S FLOOR MAKES EVERYTHING WORTH IT. THE YEAR BEFORE THAT WHEN I WAS BEING BORN IN A JAPANESE
FACTORY I HAD NO IDEA THIS WOULD BE A POSSIBILITY.

JUST BEFORE I GO, A FEW SMALL PIECES OF ADVICE: IF YOU ARE CURRENTLY SAD, DON'T WORRY AS THINGS ARE MORE LIKELY TO GET BETTER THAN WORSE!
SCHOOL DOESN'T LAST FOREVER AND CIRCUMSTANCES CAN CHANGE IN AN INCREDIBLE WAY OVER THE COURSE OF A YEAR.
DON'T TRUST SQUIRRELS. DRINK LOTS OF WATER. ASK LOTS OF QUESTIONS. KEEP GOOD FRIENDS CLOSE. DON'T RACE A GIRAFFE.
OH AND WHEN THE OPPORTUNITY COMES UP, PLEASE DON'T MOVE TO MARS. IT'S DUSTY AND THERE ISN'T ANYTHING TO DO THERE.
IT'S BEEN GREAT CHATTING WITH YOU. I WISH I HAD MORE TIME. I'M GOING TO RETURN TO SITTING QUIETLY NOW.

THANKS FOR LISTENING.

LION

1.
LIONESS WHERE ARE YOU? LIONESS?! SHE WENT OUT TO FETCH SOME OF PHIL'S CEREAL CRUMBS AND NEVER RETURNED!

2.
SHE'S NOT IN THIS PLANT WHY DO HUMANS BRING GIANT TREES INTO THEIR HOMES? LUDICROUS.

3.
SHE'S NOT IN DAN AND PHIL'S SINK NEXT TO THE SHAVER. WHY DO HUMANS SHAVE THEIR MANES? I AM PROUD OF MINE.

4.
I'D CHECK THE SHOWER BUT PHIL IS CURRENTLY IN IT SINGING 'MY HEART WILL GO ON'. REMIND ME TO BLEACH MY EYES LATER.

5.
LION, HELP!

6.
HELP ME!!

7.
I'LL SAVE YOU, LIONESS!

8.
TAKE THIS!

9.
LION, YOU KILLED DARREN!

I THOUGHT YOU WERE IN DANGER?

10.
NO. WE JUST NEEDED HELP DECIDING WHAT MOVIE TO RENT!

11.
OOPS.

12.
RIP DARREN.

THE LIFE AND TIMES OF SIMON THE SHRIMP

P: Did you know that I became a father in 2011? A father to a prehistoric pet created from powder, but a father nonetheless. This pet was Simon the shrimp. It didn't feel right writing a book without featuring this little guy. He changed a lot of lives and inspired many people to live life to the fullest. Let's go back to the beginning.

BIRTH

IT ALL STARTED ON CHRISTMAS DAY 2010 WHEN I OPENED SOME 'PREHISTORIC TRIOPS' FROM SANTA! TRIOPS ARE INCREDIBLY WEIRD CRUSTACEANS THAT YOU CAN GROW FROM POWDER. ON 23 JANUARY I DECIDED TO GIVE BIRTH TO THESE LITTLE MONSTERS WITH THE HELP OF DAN! THIS IS THE MOMENT THAT LIFE WAS CREATED! I FELT SO POWERFUL:

AFTER A COUPLE OF DAYS THEY GREW INTO TRIOPS! THESE CREATURES WERE FASCINATING BUT ALSO GROSS. THEY WOULD CONSTANTLY FIGHT TO THE DEATH AND EAT EACH OTHER. THEY'D ALSO DO SIT-UPS ON THE BOTTOM OF THE TANK IN A RACE AGAINST TIME TO SHED THEIR EXOSKELETONS BEFORE DROWNING.

AFTER SEEING HOW GROTESQUE THE CREATURES HAD BECOME DAN DECIDED TO ABANDON ALL SENSE OF DUTY AND I BECAME A SINGLE FATHER. ONE BY ONE THE TRIOPS FOUGHT TO THE DEATH IN A MINIATURE WATERY HUNGER GAMES UNTIL ONE TRIOP REMAINED, BUT HE WASN'T ALONE IN THE TANK ...

INTERESTINGLY THE TRIOPS' FOOD CONTAINED 'FAIRY SHRIMP' EGGS. AND AS THE FINAL TRIOP DIED IN A FATAL SET OF SIT-UPS A COUPLE OF THE SHRIMP SURVIVED! IT WAS TIME TO WELCOME SIMON INTO THE WORLD.

MEMEMEMEMEMEMEME

OVER THE NEXT WEEK SIMON WENT FROM STRENGTH TO STRENGTH AND GREW INTO A BACKFLIPPING SUPER SHRIMP. WHILST THE TRIOPS SEEMED LIKE RAMPAGING MINDLESS ALIENS, YOU COULD REALLY SEE A KIND SOUL BEHIND HIS EYES. IF ONLY THAT SOUL KNEW HOW MUCH IT WAS APPRECIATED.

OVER THE NEXT FEW MONTHS, 'SIMON FEVER' HIT THE INTERNET. HE CREATED HUGE WAVES OF LOVE BOTH ONLINE AND OFFLINE. I HAD REQUESTS FOR SIMON T-SHIRTS AND PLUSHIES AND SOMEONE EVEN EMAILED ME ASKING IF HE'D CONSIDER DATING A HUMAN. IT WAS A WEIRD TIME.

HE GREW AND GREW AND GREW AND EVENTUALLY IMPREGNATED HIS TANKMATE LINDA WHO EITHER DEVELOPED EGG SACS OR TUMOURS ON HER BODY, WE WERE NEVER ENTIRELY SURE.

UNFORTUNATELY THIS HAPPINESS COULDN'T LAST FOREVER ...

THE DEATH OF SIMON

ON 4 MAY 2011 SIMON MOVED ON TO THE GIANT SHRIMP TANK IN THE SKY. THE INTERNET HAD A COUPLE OF DAYS OF MOURNING AND MANY FAMOUS FACES TURNED UP AT HIS SHRIMP FUNERAL.

AFTER A BEAUTIFUL AND MOVING SERVICE HE MOVED ONTO HIS FINAL RESTING PLACE.

London apartment

D: Here we are. Our pad in the big smoke!

P: Neither of us have ever called it that.

D: Too late to start? So London! Why would we choose to move from lovely little very cold Manchester down to this crazy giant busy city?

P: I feel like we'd both kind of 'done' Manchester by then? I mean you'd been there for two years but I grew up there and I went every weekend!

D: Yeah we liked it but it was time to go somewhere new. Plus literally everyone we knew in real life lived in London and we wanted to try actually having friends.

P: That's because instead of socialising with other students at University you only talked to people on the internet.

D: I regret nothing.

P: Yup it was scary but we felt like it was the right thing to do! We started working with Radio 1, all the people that made videos lived in the same place and we both felt like we needed to take that big jump.

D: You mean utterly terrifying freefall into a strange land where we had no experience?

P: Yeah!

D: Again I feel like we were ridiculously lucky getting this apartment. We spent an entire week getting lost around London, looking at places that were all horrible!

P: Like that one that became available 'as the landlord left', which we think meant that the old lady who used to live in it died.

D: I felt like she died in the armchair in the lounge, which would explain the mysterious stain.

P: We learned a lot of lessons about places looking better in photos on the website. One place even had chairs that turned out to be painted polystyrene.

D: Then there was the time we got lost in Shadwell and you thought you were going to die.

P: Thanks for bringing that up, Dan. We did find a place in the end though and it is awesome! Even if it was totally unfurnished when we moved in and all we had was boxes and a beanbag.

D: Yes we had to buy a lot of cheap furniture and learn to assemble it very quickly! Which might explain why literally all of it fell apart in the first two months.

D: Two years later though we're settled with well-built furniture and we're proper Londoners.

P: I'll never forget my wild Northern roots!

London apartment

DAN'S ROOM

D: The main reason we picked this place is because the bedrooms are gigantic! Most of the bedrooms in London were like tiny coffins, but as people who never go outside we needed a big hamster cage.

P: Yeah now we have enough room each to sleep, film videos and do aerobics.

D: You have literally never done an 'aerobic'.

P: But I could! I would like the reader to know that I just did a star jump.

D: Congratulations. My bedroom also had an old piano in it which I was told hasn't been moved since the house was built 100 years ago.

P: I bet it has ghosts in it.

D: Don't ruin my bedroom. Also that desk is where I am writing these very words that you're reading!

P: Dan! I told you to stop breaking the fourth page.

PHIL'S ROOM

P: My room also came with a piece of furniture! Not a ghost piano though. A giant bed made entirely out of wicker.

D: Literally, it's like a gigantic picnic basket, it's pretty hideous.

P: I mean I don't want to offend whoever weaved my bed, but the only reason I kept it is I couldn't work out how to get it through my doorway.

HALLWAY

P: Good hallway! Nice light walls that we have destroyed by banging chairs and camera equipment against them.

D: Do you think there's any chance we'll get our deposit back?

P: We've destroyed this place so much we'll probably have to buy the whole thing.

D: Also good carpet for lying on if you're having a crisis.

KITCHEN

D: This bloody door. You'd think the idea of a completely glass door leading in to your kitchen sounds nice and fancy! No. It's a death trap.

P: Pretty much every night when the lights are turned off the glass door just turns into an invisible wall of pain. My nose is twitching just remembering all of the incidents.

LOUNGE

D: I was just excited to have a fireplace!

P: I don't trust gas fires. I don't really understand how they work, so I'm constantly afraid I'm going to blow up the whole of London every time there's a cold morning.

D: This is also probably the geekiest room in existence. There isn't a single surface that isn't covered with some kind of TV or game merchandise.

P: I'd have it no other way!

D: Then we have our trusty sofa where we spend 99% of our lives. I think initially I crushed the sofa cushion into the shape of my spine, but now I've spent so much time slouching on it my spine has moulded to fit the sofa crease.

OFFICE

D: The totally random third floor of our apartment which is just one little square room.

P: For over a year when we moved in this was only known as the 'room of shame'. It was the place we threw all of our boxes of stuff from Manchester but as time went on we only added to it with all the cardboard boxes from the furniture we bought.

D: Turns out it's quite a cool little cave for putting our computers! Add in one sofa bed for guests and a couple of funky cushions and, voilà, you have a gaming channel zone!

P: I'm glad it has a purpose now. I always feel bad for an unused room. Now it's the home of all our geeky videos and cooperative rage.

TOILET

D: So one of our viewers kindly decided to give us a door-length One Direction poster as a moving-in gift. We had no idea where to put it for ages until we decided to stick it to the inside of the toilet door.

P: There is about 10cm of room between the door and your face when sat on the toilet, so the idea of forcing our guests to stare at a giant grinning Harry Styles head was very funny.

D: We always look forward to the loud 'what the?!' when someone sees it for the first time. Oh the things those boys have seen in there.

STAIRS

D: Our apartment is technically on the third floor but because it's so weird everything's actually on the fourth!

P: We nearly died moving in. Imagine carrying a flatpack sofa up four flights of stairs during the hottest August England has ever had.

D: I honestly think it's the closest I've ever come to dying from exhaustion. I remember us lying on the floor panting for at least an hour. Though without these stairs we'd literally never exercise so we're begrudgingly grateful!

P: Thank you death-stairs.

SECRET STAIRCASE

D: And down here is the secret staircase to the sub-apartment!

P: This is where we keep things like our 'red room', the portal from the old apartment and our team of monkeys that are writing this book for us.

D: PHIL, STOP THEY KNOW TOO MUCH. ABORT! ABORT! PAGE OVER

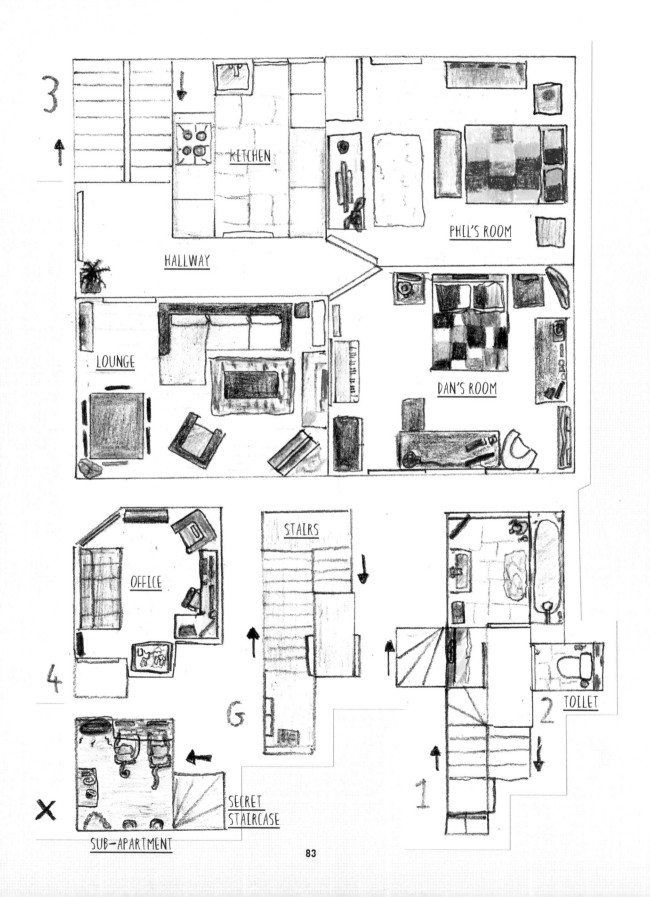

3

KETCHEN

HALLWAY

PHIL'S ROOM

LOUNGE

DAN'S ROOM

OFFICE

STAIRS

4

G

TOILET

2

1

X

SECRET STAIRCASE

SUB-APARTMENT

83

WHICH PHIL AND DAN DINING CHAIR ARE YOU?

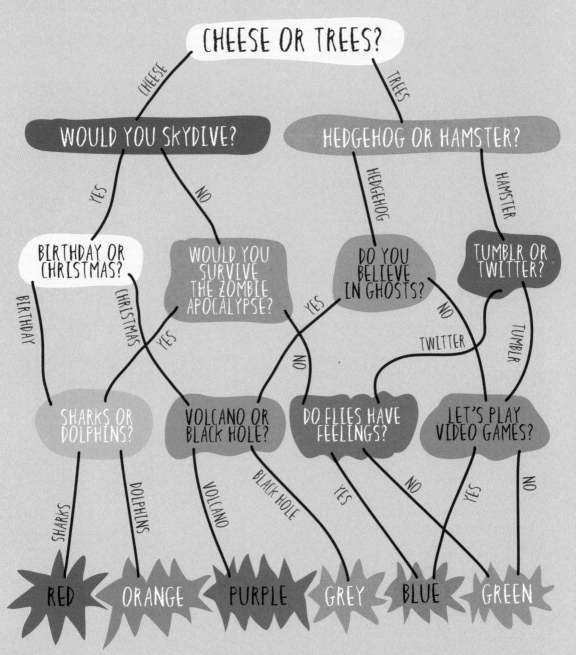

CHEESE OR TREES?

CHEESE → WOULD YOU SKYDIVE?

TREES → HEDGEHOG OR HAMSTER?

WOULD YOU SKYDIVE?
YES → BIRTHDAY OR CHRISTMAS?
NO → WOULD YOU SURVIVE THE ZOMBIE APOCALYPSE?

HEDGEHOG → DO YOU BELIEVE IN GHOSTS?

HAMSTER → TUMBLR OR TWITTER?

BIRTHDAY OR CHRISTMAS?
BIRTHDAY → SHARKS OR DOLPHINS?
CHRISTMAS → VOLCANO OR BLACK HOLE?

WOULD YOU SURVIVE THE ZOMBIE APOCALYPSE?
YES → SHARKS OR DOLPHINS?
NO → DO FLIES HAVE FEELINGS?

DO YOU BELIEVE IN GHOSTS?
YES → VOLCANO OR BLACK HOLE?
NO → LET'S PLAY VIDEO GAMES?

TUMBLR OR TWITTER?
TWITTER → DO FLIES HAVE FEELINGS?
TUMBLR → LET'S PLAY VIDEO GAMES?

SHARKS OR DOLPHINS?
SHARKS → RED
DOLPHINS → ORANGE

VOLCANO OR BLACK HOLE?
VOLCANO → PURPLE
BLACK HOLE → GREY

DO FLIES HAVE FEELINGS?
YES → GREY
NO → BLUE

LET'S PLAY VIDEO GAMES?
YES → BLUE
NO → GREEN

RED   ORANGE   PURPLE   GREY   BLUE   GREEN

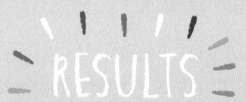

RESULTS

ATTENTION! THIS IS SET IN STONE.
YOU CAN NEVER RE-TAKE THE CHAIR QUIZ.

GREY:
You are the grey chair! Dark, mysterious and slightly sinister. You share a spiritual bond with Dan and would choose a leather coat over a fluffy jumper. There is a small chance you are a vampire and you are probably hiding a huge secret, unfortunately you can't tell anyone as you are a chair.

BLUE:
You are the blue chair! Sorry that 90% of your life is taken up by Phil's butt. You prefer walks by the beach to crazy nightclubs. Sometimes you sneeze and blink at the same time which is meant to be impossible (don't tell the government or they will experiment on you). You would make a great rocket scientist, dog groomer or FBI agent, unfortunately that is not possible as you are a chair.

RED:
You are the red chair! You are outgoing, loud and you like the smell of bonfires. You think with your heart before your head and cats don't tend to trust you. You'd make a great wedding planner, storm trooper or ice sculptor. Unfortunately chairs can't sculpt so you will remain in Dan and Phil's lounge with unfulfilled dreams.

ORANGE:
You are the orange chair! Dan's chair of choice. He leans back on you quite a lot so there is a high chance you are clumsier than most. You are very indecisive and it takes you way too long to get ready in the morning. You would be a great ice-cream tester, emu analyst or president. Unfortunately chairs are banned from general elections so you will have to stay in the dining room.

PURPLE:
You are the purple chair! You have been sat on by the butts of various Dan and Phil apartment guests including Anthony Padilla, Charlie McDonnell and Tyler Oakley. You are highly psychic and can summon ghosts with a sneeze. Your lucky number is eight and your patronus is Samara from *The Ring*. You like scented candles, shrines and secret doorways. Unfortunately, chairs can't walk so you will never get to go through them. Sad times.

GREEN:
You are the green chair! Dan and Phil don't have enough friends to fill their entire dining table so you are the outsider of the group. You are at one with nature and animals love you. You frequently talk to yourself and have a lot of creativity. You'd prefer a movie night with your best friend to a banana boat ride. You'd be a great zoo-keeper, hamster breeder or dolphin psychiatrist but unfortunately chairs can't swim so go back to being never sat on.

Phil's hamster breeding page

So you want to breed hamsters?!
YOU CAME TO THE RIGHT PAGE!

This page will fulfil every hamstery need you have. Even if you don't want to breed a hamster, come learn something!

Oh? You want some context? Okay.

The Hamster Ball of Context

For a lot of my school life my nickname was 'hamster boy'. Not because I looked like one. Well I did kind of look like one but that's beside the point. I was the school's infamous hamster breeder!

It all started when I spent half my life begging my parents for a chinchilla or a rat. I almost got close to owning the chinchilla of destiny until my mum googled them and found out they can run up walls and hop up to 3m high. She is also afraid of rats and their tails (totally ratist) so to make me shut up my parents bought me a male hamster (Norris) and a female (Phoebe) with the hope of breeding them and selling the babies!

Interesting Hamster Facts

* Syrian hamsters are solitary creatures! They love their own space and will fight to the DEATH if you put them in a cage together. It's like a fluffy Mortal Kombat.

* Hamsters are colour blind so if Morpheus offered them a blue or a red pill they would probably just bite his hand.

* Male hamsters are called boars and females are called sows.

* One human year is equivalent to 25 hamster years! So make sure you prepare 25 individual birthday parties a year.

* Hamsters can see for a distance of six inches so they probably just think you are a magical pair of hands rather than a human.

* Hamsters are both telepathic and telekinetic.

How to Tame a Hamster

Okay this may sound weird but I would get into the bath with my hamsters. FULLY CLOTHED (!!) NO WATER. I'd bring their food bowl and wear cricket gloves so they couldn't bite me and just let them run on my legs and hands to get used to me as a human! I would then keep returning them to the food bowl if they walked too far away from it and they would then trust me and associate me with snacks. I appreciate this is a very weird mental image but it WORKS.

How to Breed a Hamster

First, set up a tiny romantic meal and play some high-pitched Barry White music.

The female hamster gets in the mood for hamster lovin' every four days. So you may be lucky and they'll do it first time or you'll have a fluffy Mortal Kombat situation for the other three days. You'll realise it's going to happen as the female hamster goes completely flat like she's been run over by a small tractor and doesn't want to kill the male.

Then just give them a few moments of privacy. (I held up a small cardboard screen as the miracle of nature happened.) Just remember to remove the male before they fight again!

Pregnant Hamster

Your hamster will be pregnant for about 15–17 days. Once you see her start to balloon leave her alone! Just quietly fill up the food and don't play with her or put her in a ball or a hamster sky restaurant.

Birth

Hamsters can have between 3 and 12 babies (Mine had 13! Norris was like a prize stallion). You will soon hear the mewing of tiny babies. Bask in the godlike feeling of creating new life. DO NOT DISTURB THE NEST OR PICK UP THE BABIES! This causes a Hamsterball Lecter style situation where the mother will eat her own young. Scatter some broccoli or grated carrot for them to eat.

In about four weeks you'll be ready to separate the boys and girls into different cages and three weeks after that they are ready to be rehomed! Make sure you sell them to friendly and loving homes and enjoy your millions of pounds. (If you strap a paper horn to one and sell it to Richard Branson as a baby unicorn, that is.) (Note: This is fraud. Please don't sell false unicorns.)

My Hamsters

I can't find any more pictures of my hamsters so here is a drawing:

Kevin, Barry, Buffy, Spike, Tom, Jerry, Treacle, Badger, Snowball, Lucy, Winston, Mouse and Fluff

Disclaimer: Even though I consider myself a hamster pro, you should probably consult experts before embarking upon your own hamster adventures.

Why Phil Can't Have a Hamster

Look, okay, I'm not a bad guy.

PHIL JUST CAN'T HAVE A HAMSTER.

Here are the reasons:

1. It's against our tenancy agreement. I know Phil keeps saying he'll hide it in his wardrobe but that's not a long-term solution.

2. We travel too much and have no friends. Who could we leave it with when we fly off to a YouTube convention or to do some video job? He can't mail it to his family up north! Until we have robot maids that can feed and water pets, we're just away too much.

3. It would be too noisy. I know very well the horror of a hamster chewing the metal bars of its cage at 3am when you haven't slept for a week. Also, how can we film videos with cage clanking and wheel squeaking in the background?! Don't tell me it'd be a cute background noise, we all know it isn't true.

4. Hamsters are unbelievably smelly. If how well Phil maintains the state of our kitchen and how often he cleans it are anything to go by this would not work out well for our noses. We've already filled our apartment with a dangerous amount of scented candles and the fire hazard required to out-smell a hamster is not something I want to risk.

5. Moral boundaries. Those familiar with the story of my hamster Suki will know that I do not underestimate the intelligence of small fuzzy rodents and how much they grasp the true nature of existence in this universe and freedom. Sure you might get a dumb one that happily wheels itself dizzy for ten hours a day and then sleeps, but what if I have to deal with another freakishly intelligent one?! I can't bear to make the decision between trapping something against its will and letting it brave the harsh reality of nature. I mean, come on, we live in London, it'll get eaten by a giant rat in two minutes

Conclusion

I'm sorry, Phil, it's not personal, but at the moment we just can't get a hamster. I hope this page has convinced some of you why I feel the need to make this decision, but I believe it is the right one. Perhaps one day soon Phil will have a garden or his own home and he can turn it into the hamster-breeding paradise of his dreams. He's a weird guy, isn't he?

DAN AND PHIL ON BBC RADIO 1

D: So, we have an actual radio show on the BBC.

P: Well you're saying that now, Dan, we might have been totally fired whenever this is being read.

D: To be fair that is a definite possibility. So how on earth did this all happen?

P: Well the story of us and the BBC goes all the way back to 2011! Two peeps called Laura-May and Alistair working at Radio 1 were putting together a talent show they were doing live in Edinburgh. They thought it'd be interesting to get someone to perform on webcam, so they looked on the internet and decided it'd be cool and forward-thinking to invite a vlogger. For some reason they decided we were the ones they wanted to contact!

D: I'm shocked you didn't scare them off for 100 reasons.

P: Maybe they liked the weirdness?

D: The only possible explanation. I'm not sure what talent they thought you could perform? Talking to camera?

P: That's basically the one thing I'm good at, but you're right! I had no idea what to do and I was already terrified so I asked if Dan could join me to make it easier and they said yes.

D: So then we had to decide on an 'act', and what did we choose to do? The 'blindfolded cat-face game'. Yes, we were just going to draw a cat on each other's faces. I have no idea what we were thinking.

P: I can't believe this led us to getting a radio show.

D: The day came and we were watching the livestream of the show with hundreds of people in a room watching all kinds of jugglers and magicians and people with, y'know, actual talents. Then they introduced us.

P: The internet connection was so terrible that we basically looked like 15 yellow pixels and Nick Grimshaw forgot Dan's name.

D: If I recall, he kept calling me 'the one in the black t-shirt'.

P: So we did our game, which Dan totally cheated on by the way – you can see his eyes open.

D: Hey it was an accident! I only glanced. And yes three minutes of uncomfortable face-touching noises was our debut on British radio.

P: I lost so my forfeit was to get a plate of whipped cream smacked into my face which completely ruined the clothes I was wearing as they never stopped smelling like mouldy cheese. However, afterwards we were told so many of our followers tried to watch the stream that we actually broke the website!

D: We are the original internet Godzillas, Phil and I. Don't let us near any tiny website or we'll accidentally crush it like a clumsy giant.

P: This weird talent show incident apparently got people talking at the BBC, as one day we got a fateful email from a man named Joe.

D: Right out of nowhere they asked if we wanted to come down to London to discuss making a radio show. We kind of freaked out.

P: It was terrifying but really exciting! I remember walking past Gary Barlow on the way into the Radio 1 building and reaching for my phone to scream at my mum before remembering that's probably not acceptable behaviour.

D: We felt like the two biggest dorks in the world walking through this cool crazy office with our weird haircuts.

P: We were the biggest dorks in the world.

D: Oh definitely. So we met up with the guys we'd been emailing and they said 'how would you like a two-hour video show on the radio on Christmas day?' Two hours of music and video weirdness from us beamed across the world on the radio and in video on the website on the most magical day of the year. The worst/best idea ever.

P: We then spent about two months wrestling with crazy microphone equipment, inflatable sharks and balloons filled with flour to make what became the AmazingPhil and Danisnotonfire Christmas show on Radio 1.

Dan & Phil on Webcam

Dan & Phil 2011 show

D: It was pretty amazing. I remember my family gathering around the TV in the lounge not at all understanding how a radio show could be watched. It was a weird Christmas day as I spent most of it shaking with nerves.

P: We were proud of our first radio baby! And apparently so were the BBC as they actually emailed us back. The next time they contacted us they wanted us to do a documentary on internet dating as they figured we know stuff about the internet.

D: I don't think either of us are really experts in online dating. We rose to the challenge, however, and made a wonderfully strange documentary about love on the internet which involved me calling a TV celebrity property expert called Sarah Beeny to tell her how to install Skype. I still have her mobile number.

P: Fast forward to summer and apparently they liked us enough to give us another Christmas show for 2012! This was one of the final pushes that convinced us to make our leap of faith and move to London.

D: Though this time it was just a one-hour show instead of two so maybe they liked us half as much?

P: Well obviously not, as at the start of December, right in the middle of crafting our second hour-long audiovisual special, the bomb was dropped.

D: Out of nowhere we got a message from the big boss asking us to make a formal pilot for a full-time radio show. He wanted us to take over the old format of

The Request Show where people call in to request songs and make it a big Dan and Phil internet video explosion.

P: This was on top of the Christmas show we were making, our own YouTube videos and everything else we had going on, including Christmas!

D: We got it done though and sent it off, then a few days before Christmas we were invited to the BBC and got told the news. We'd have our own Dan and Phil show on actual BBC Radio 1!

P: It was mental – neither of us could believe it at all! Then they told us they wanted us to start in the first week of the new year.

D: Not only did we have to get everything for the show prepared in time, we had to learn how to actually be radio DJs! Usually people spend years practising in their spare time, on student radio, and on 4am shifts for your local Jazz station, but us? We were given less than two weeks.

P: Now I'm not a very coordinated guy. I don't drive because I can't multitask and I'm 100% sure I can't be trusted with other people's lives. A radio desk is like a rocket ship.

D: There are about 4,000 buttons that all do different, powerful and terrifying things and any one of them could blow up the BBC. The multitasking of 'driving the desk' and presenting is a challenge in itself, but then we obviously had to go and create what I honestly think is the most complicated radio show of all time. First of all it was a request show, so it was completely unpredictable. We couldn't plan any timings as anyone could choose any song and the callers could talk for as long as they liked. Also we had to stand up which made it super awkward to press buttons or look at notes as we were told 'all the best DJs are standing now, it's just better energy'. Couple in our ridiculously complicated games like 'Fan Wars' that had us juggling two callers, two possible winning songs and six sound effects ready to go. Then the cherry on the cake – the whole thing was live on camera. We were very jealous of the other DJs whose shows were mainly sitting in a chair looking at notes when you need them and casually having banter with your pals. Our show was like a rave filled with barnyard animals set on fire.

P: And a beautiful flaming animal party it was.

D: There was only so much preparation we could do before the time came for our first live show.

P: I don't think I slept for about three days due to nerves and even though we came into the BBC every day to practise I felt like a flailing octopus made of jelly.

D: The first show. What a crazy story. Firstly, we had no time to prepare as everyone in the building was coming up to us all day to wish us luck, which was ironically the least helpful thing at that moment.

P: Then just before we went on we were told we had to swap studios so we wouldn't be able to chill out in one until we went live, instead we had to wait for the chart show to finish and walk in during the final song. This changed the plan. My worst thing ever is changing the plan.

D: I don't think the people doing the chart show fully appreciated how much we were internally freaking out as we were carrying the cameras and our laptops in our hands as they leisurely picked up their coats with only one minute left of the final song.

P: We managed to log into the computers, plug everything in, stand up and with about 20 seconds left we were in position. 'Hi we are Dan' 'And Phil!' 'And you're listening to BBC Radio 1!' Then the camera fell off its tripod. We are not joking, it snapped.

D: During our first live link on the radio, of course it would happen to us! Joe Harland – one of the most important men at the BBC then ran into the room and spent the first five minutes holding it up trying to be as still as possible until we played our first song.

P: The next two hours were the slowest and fastest, craziest hours of my life, but we did it.

D: At the end I had nothing left. It's like I had completely exhausted all the energy in my body, mind and soul. We had no idea how it went but then everyone came into the studio and congratulated us! We sat around with our team and had a giant cake and that was the first Dan and Phil show on Radio 1. The rest is history.

Dan & Phil in the studio

Aftermath of the first show

HOW'S IT DIFFERENT TO VIDEOS?

D: Lots of people ask us how doing live radio compares to YouTube.

P: Honestly it's pretty much the same! We're just having funny entertaining conversations about things, but instead of having to sit and edit it then put it on the internet, it happens live!

D: Which is fun and also terrifying. I can't believe I haven't accidentally sworn yet.

P: At the end of the day there are different skills like video editing or pressing buttons on a complicated desk, but the only difference is saying 'And up next on Radio 1 it's Britney Spears'!

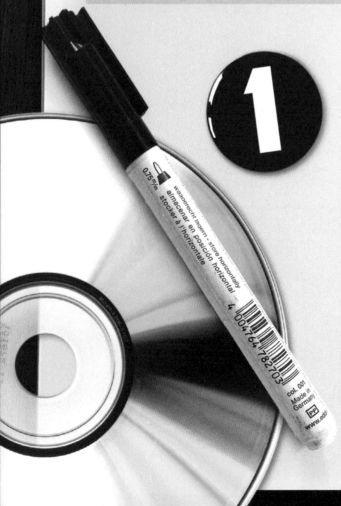

THE DAN AND PHIL SHOW FEATURES

Internet News - We read out all the weirdest and wonderful news stories we found on the internet that week that regular radio listeners may have missed out on! It wouldn't be complete without our signature lensless 3D glasses. INTERNET NEWS *bong*

Phil scratching his ear while Dan pretends to talk

Dan vs. Phil - Every week for over a year we came up with a new embarrassing, physically degrading challenge to attempt against each other live on camera. From putting our hands in Wellington boots and jumping over obstacles like horses, to crawling across floors in sleeping bags like caterpillars, the lowest moments of our lives were streamed for the world to laugh at.

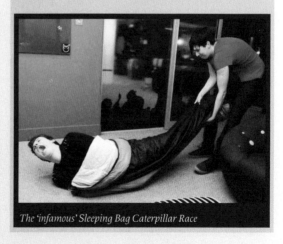

The 'infamous' Sleeping Bag Caterpillar Race

Fan Wars - The idea was to pit two fan bases against each other live on the radio for the right to have their artist's song played. Two live callers have to compete at a mystery challenge that could be gargling the song, animal impressions or our favourite 'Noise Treasure Hunt', where they had to run around their house making noises. Incredible chaos.

Sorry I Don't Know How To Internet - Laughing at people that can't use technology. Basically. In a nice consensual way though! People sent in stories of their elderly relatives or friends not knowing how to do basic computer tasks for all the people who spend their lives on the internet to chuckle about.

The Intenserviews - From our very first Christmas show where we made Tim Westwood build a reindeer out of Play-Doh, we have forced people to answer ridiculous questions as quickly as possible whilst enduring some kind of distraction. From Radio DJs to popstars and vloggers, many people have gone through this trial.

The 7 Second Challenge - We turned Phil's YouTube phenomenon into 'The most intense-per-second radio feature of all time', attempting to do whatever the other person says in a ridiculously short amount of time. We play the 7 Second Challenge live on the radio and the winner picks a song of their choice!

AWARD WINNERS

P: Did you know our show is actually Academy Award-winning? Okay it's from the UK's Radio Academy, but fancy and serious nonetheless!

D: It was actually the people's choice award, but I guess depending on how you look at it it's either the least important award or the only one that actually means anything!

P: That was a terrifying serious evening filled with crazy famous presenters and suspiciously energetic performers. Dan also offended a professional footballer.

P: Then afterwards we went out to a crazy celebrity club and ended up falling asleep on Nick Grimshaw's floor with his dog.

D: I think that world isn't meant for us. We're definitely 'stay inside on the internet in pyjamas' kind of guys.

Our golden headphones! You can't wear them as they're made of steel

CRAZY EVENTS!

D: I don't know why, but Radio 1 let us out of our apartments and the tiny studio into the real world to actually interact with famous bands and popstars.

P: I always found it terrifying. I liked to think we offered a unique form of entertainment that the fans of the artists wouldn't usually find!

D: That's one way of putting it! Yep, from our first event with the infamous story of One Direction to going on stage at a festival I attended as a teenager, we have a lot of memories ...

Introducing Imagine Dragons on stage to a billion people

*Teen Awards 2013:
Dan and Taylor Swift draw each other blindfolded*

*Big Weekend 2013 Londonderry:
The 'Legenderry Quiz' videos we had one minute each to film*

*Reading Festival 2013:
Our 'InTENTerviews' inside a tent covered with creepy fanart*

*Big Weekend 2014: Dan eats a satsuma on stage behind
One Direction*

Teen Awards 2014: Ariana Grande gives Phil her cat-ear tiara after they drew each other

#Dick

Phil makes a show with Joss Whedon and he signs Phil's Buffy comic!

Music Played

Add music you love and enjoy it with **BBC** *playlister*

Muse
Uprising
WARNERS BROS.

Kanye West
All Of The Lights (feat. Rihanna & Kid Cudi)
MY BEAUTIFUL DARK TWISTED FANTASY. DEF JAM.

All Time Low
Weightless
HOPELESS RECORDS.

Katy Perry
Last Friday Night (t.g.i.f.)
VIRGIN.

Coldplay
Every Teardrop Is A Waterfall
PARLOPHONE.

Justin Bieber
Little Drummer Boy (feat. Busta Rhymes)
MERCURY.

Britney Spears
Toxic
TOXIC. JIVE.

Fall Out Boy
Thanks For The Memories
THANKS FOR THE MEMORIES. MERCURY.

Beyoncé
Party
MUSIC WORLD / COLUMBIA.

Shivaree
Goodnight Moon
I OUGHTTA GIVE YOU A SHOT IN THE HEAD FOR MAKING ME LIVE IN THIS DUMP. EMI.

iamamiwhoami
t
D.E.F.

Green Day
Holiday
HOLIDAY. REPRISE. 16.

Cornelia Funke
Now and Hereafter
BY THE FIRE / NOW AND HEREAFTER. CAMP MOZART.

Kreayshawn
Gucci Gucci

The xx
Crystalised
YOUNG TURKS.

Rebecca Black
Friday
ARK MUSIC FACTORY.

Our first ever show's playlist!

THE TIME WE MET ONE DIRECTION

BBC RADIO 1 TEEN AWARDS 2012 –
A DANK CORRIDOR IN WEMBLEY ARENA, LONDON,
OCTOBER 7TH.

D: In the year before we were given our Radio show, Phil and I, as up-and-coming video makers for Radio 1, were asked if we wanted to interview some 'guests' at the upcoming Teen Awards!

P: This was terrifying because, other than a couple of awkward moments with Bring Me The Horizon's Oli Sykes and some people who we grabbed when they happened to be at the BBC during the recording of one of our Christmas shows, this would be the first time we'd ever done something 'professional' at a big serious event.

D: In typical Dan and Phil fashion we started preparing the night before the event.

P: You mean typical Dan fashion. I wanted to prepare three weeks before but you spent several days staring at the carpet thinking about a video.

D: This is conjecture.

P: Dan, you were procasti-

D: Phil, you're ruining the flow of the story.

P: ...

D: The night before any big event we 'work' at, even to this day, feels a bit like we're Katniss and Peeta.

Above images, left to right:
Us with Oli Sykes.
Us with Tim Westwood
Us with McFly

P: Don't say Katniss and Peeta.

D: ...two clones of Katniss the night before The Hunger Games.

P: I'm not sure if playing games with popstars is the same as having to survive a battle arena filled with trained death machines.

D: Well, if you think about it ...

P: Okay, I'll continue the story. Our last-minute preparation meant that we didn't have an opportunity to write our questions on the super-professional-looking folded pieces of A4 until we were in the car on the way to the arena. I don't like looking at things in a moving car!

D: Phil gets motion sickness if he blinks for too long and sees his eyelids while moving.

P: Thanks. So we were desperately scribbling with permanent markers ...

D: ... which made my entire hand pitch-black because of my left-handed handicap. Very professional looking.

P: ... and trying to mentally prepare ourselves. But one thing was sticking at the front of our brains: we were told we might meet One Direction.

D: Now, I understand these events are crazy and you can never guarantee an artist will turn up. People might not have time, or someone could be a diva and not like the colour of a carpet, but YOU CAN'T JUST TELL SOMEONE THEY 'might' MEET ONE DIRECTION.

P: 1D in 2012 were literally the most talked-about people on the entire planet; it's when the internet has been at its craziest for anything to do with them, so not only were our scary bosses like, 'We know what you do with them will be great!' but we knew whatever we did would be watched by millions of Directioners online.

D: You could say this added to our concerningly rapidly rising anxiety levels.

The ravenous horde assembles

P: A bit.

D: Maybe. And what were we greeted with when we arrived at the arena? A pulsating, frothing ocean of thousands of screaming One Direction fans.

P: It was like a thousand of those screaming firework rockets going off at the same time, all the time. Or like being in a room with a billion excited bees.

D: The ground actually shook. I'm convinced that that amount of high-frequency noise must affect the tectonic plates somehow. Either way, no cat in a four-mile radius must have lived through that evening without exploding.

P: And then we were taken to the 'crew entrance' – if you're expecting anything to do with TV or radio to be glitzy, you'll be disappointed. It was like a *Saw* trap.

D: Slight exaggeration.

P: It was like the kind of scary concrete basement a *Saw* trap would be in! Just without the pointy death machine.

D: That's true. And my god, was the atmosphere ABSOLUTELY TERRIFYING. We were being shepherded down tight corridors with flickering lights, and every now and then there would be this terrifying wave of noise, where reverberating screams would literally shake dust off the exposed pipes above us.

P: Kind of like Katniss getting bombed in District 13.

D: Let the *Hunger Games* metaphors go, Phil. Now this kind of hectic atmosphere is what we learned dressing rooms were for. If you are a fancy presenter or a popstar, who has to practise something or get in the zone to perform, you need a room to emotionally prepare!

P: We didn't have a room.

D: No. You see the thing is, back then we weren't really known to a lot of people at Radio 1. We weren't people with a proper radio show, we were just two weirdos with strange haircuts, who sometimes loitered awkwardly in the corner of their office, talking about stuff for their 'YouTube channel'. This was back when YouTube was still seen as a place only for weirdos and cats.

P: We were and definitely are still weirdos.

D: I'm not denying this. So when all these established radio presenters, and scary TV people were running around making their actually important stuff with their big teams before going back to their private sanctuaries, we just had to stand awkwardly in a corner eating the crisps we stuffed into Phil's backpack.

P: We were at least excited to see the backstage area where we'd film these interview videos though!

D: Ah yes, the toilets.

P: They weren't just toilets.

D: Pretty much.

P: It was more like a mix between a laundry cupboard and a World War Two bunker that happened to have toilets in them. We were told that all the dressing rooms and free spaces were occupied, and this was the only area left.

D: The room was in total the size of an average car. There was more room in the actual toilets themselves and one of the presenters, Matt Edmondson, decided to actually film his interviews in the toilet, which meant everyone helping him was stood outside pushing us further into the wall.

P: There was one of those mirrors with the light bulbs around it though!

D: You're right, that did excite me.

P: Thankfully we were told that, if it was going to happen, 1D would be the last thing that'd happen in our day, giving us time to practise on Little Mix and Conor Maynard!

D: 'Practise on' sounds kinda weird.

'Please rescue me from these strange people.'
Conor Maynard

P: What could that even mean? Anyway it was terrifying. It's not just a nice introduction and chat, and then you spend a few relaxing moments having fun with the person. Firstly, one of their 'people' comes and they give information to another 'person', then the Senior 'person' double checks and gives us a scary look before asking exactly what we're going to do with the popstar.

D: I mean, what did it look like we were going to do?

P: You have shifty eyes, it was probably that. Then, with about 20 people crammed into this tiny, dark, kind of weird-smelling room all staring at you, wondering, 'Who are these internet people and why are they here?' the popstar walks in the room.

D: To be fair, from our experience the person themselves is usually quite happy and lovely, just not their Terminator squad that you meet before.

P: We got told by everyone, 'They only have 5 minutes, make it quick.'

D: ...when we've prepared at least 11 videos lasting an hour and a half for each person.

P: And we suddenly have to change our plans and decide exactly what we're doing.

D: That's usually when you start doing your panic face.

P: What?

D: You have this face you do when you get all panicky and flustered, and you start pacing and doing the weird hand thing –

P: Okay thanks, now I'll be self-aware forever in any kind of situation like that.

D: You're welcs, mate.

P: So after hours spent in our tiny bunker, which I'm sure was dangerously low on oxygen by that point ...

D: ... it was how I imagine being buried alive to be like. Just with more strange toilet odour coming from around the corner and people talking into bluetooth headsets.

P: ... we were told that One Direction were coming.

D: Then came probably the most amount of 'people' to check everything was okay for the group that I'd ever seen. I was concerned that if the 1D guys tried to fit in the room as well we'd be compressed into a cube of meat and die.

P: Nice vivid image. Then, when the last of the 'people' arrived he told us all the news: the guys only had ten minutes and then they had to leave, so they could only do one interview! And given the choice of the two weirdos making videos for YouTube or the actual presenter interviewing them in a toilet, who do you think they picked?

D: We were mildly heartbroken. Not just because of our preparation but because meeting One Direction would have been at that point the most popular, relevant thing we'd ever done in our entire lives.

P: The room suddenly emptied like someone blew a hole in a spaceship and an eerie silence fell.

D: They entered the room and everything went into slow motion.

P: That might have just been for you, Dan.

D: Well okay I'll tell this bit. I was blinded. A bright warm glow as if angels themselves were stroking my face ...

P: Okay I'll take over. Seriously though, they all looked so perfect! I want a stylist.

D: Pfft, you with a stylist, you know the first thing they'd do is get rid of your fringe, right?

P: I'm not ready to let go of the fringe; it's who I am.

D: It's a bit of MySpace you've been struggling to let go of since 2006 – and we both know it.

P: Anyway we were too awkward and kind of sad to do anything, so we blended in with the coat rack and watched them go off into the toilet to do the other interview.

D: We had to do something. We had it all prepared! Animal impressions, a drawing challenge, creepy questions from Tumblr I hand-sourced, I even wanted to get in a sneaky Supernote to help me win an internet competition.

P: They took so long in the toilet! It was at least fifteen minutes. I was like, 'Way to hog 1D, you boyband-warthog.'

D: Don't be mean about Matt, we like him.

P: He nearly ruined our entire lives though.

D: Nearly, but we worked it out! As they started to squeeze out of the toilet door with one of their 'people', I, in the bravest moment of my entire existence, jumped in front of the scary-headset-man and said 'hiwe'reDanand-Philwe'retwoguysfromYouTubewhomakeYouTubevideoscalledYouTubers-andwe'reherewithRadio1makingstufffortheirofficialYouTubechannelandwek-nowthe1Dfansontheinternetwouldreallyreallyreallylikeifwemadeaquickvide-owiththemIpromiseitwillonlytake1minuteplease'.
He said yes.

P: We were totally sneaky but somehow, with the man staring kinda angrily at his fancy-looking watch the whole time, we managed to film THREE videos with them!

D: Okay, let's break it down for the readers. What happened second-by-second when we met the guys.

P: It was crazy! We were four hundred per cent flustered because of Captain Serious telling us we had one minute so we awkwardly waved at them all and said, 'Hey, we're Dan and Phil, we're doing stuff for the Radio 1 YouTube!'

D: I remember Harry nodding and saying, 'Nice to meet you, Dan and Phil,' and in that moment my life was complete.

P: They were all really friendly and happy and excited! I remember thinking Niall was like a hyperactive puppy. Then, however, I started to detect a strange smell.

D: You know, I thought it might have just been the toilet room wafting over.

P: No, it was definitely in our room. I looked over to Louis and his first words to me were, 'Do you think someone farted?'

D: Wow. Was it you?

P: No, it wasn't me! Was it you?

D: No! It was probably Zayn, he's the quiet one.

P: I tried not to concentrate on it and, thankfully, it dispersed throughout the air.

D: Do you think they noticed? Is One Direction's memory of us 'the time someone farted before those two guys interviewed us'?

P: Even if it is, someone out there would be jealous of us.

D: We immediately started recording in case they were whisked away by the Terminator squad. How exactly did you end up touching Liam's head?

P: Oh yeah! The biggest world news that week was that Liam shaved his head.

D: I'm sure support hotlines had their busiest week ever and shrines dedicated to his brown hair were torn down in bereavement.

P: I just said, 'I like your hair,' and he asked me if I wanted to stroke it.

D: You do realise millions of people would probably commit unspeakable crimes to have that experience? What was it like?

P: A tall hedgehog. Or a curvy doormat.

D: You heard it here, guys. So now that we'd somehow got this opportunity we had to make the most of it. Straight in with the animal impressions, a very creative Dan and Phil content classic there.

'Like a tall hedgehog. Or a curvy doormat.'

P: I remember Louis' eagle impression was surprisingly accurate.

D: And that's coming from you! High accolades indeed.

P: Then without making it seem like we were stopping or doing anything different we got straight into the drawing challenge. Unfortunately, I only brought four pens.

D: Seriously.

P: So there was a bit of an awkward moment where Niall was stood by himself with nothing to hold. Fortunately I had a green pen in my pocket!

D: As you just magically secrete colourful stationery.

P: It's been known to happen. And then seamlessly flowing into a Supernote and some creepy questions, whilst the important man's angsty watch tapping got faster. We did it!

D: As soon as we blinked to symbolise the video finishing, the guy was like, 'RIGHT OKAY LET'S GO,' but we hadn't gotten a picture. Don't judge us, okay, even if you have the least interest in One Direction ever, you'd want a photo with them. I said don't judge us!

P: We thought the moment was lost when our friend Laura-May, like she was diving on a grenade, jumped in front of the man and said, 'Quick picture for the Twitter page!'

D: It wasn't for their Twitter. It was for us. Thank you, dear friend.

P: And with that, our crazy day was over!

D: We just kind of sank against the wall trying to process all the sensory input from probably the most insane day of our lives so far. Squeezing through the shaking concrete corridors like the intestines of a terrifying giant, we pooped out into the parking lot and got in a car on the way home.

P: I made sure to open the window and not look at anything on this car journey.

D: When we arrived back at our apartment we ordered a pizza and both slept for about 14 and a half hours. That was the time we met One Direction.

blindfolded portraits

Dan's drawing
of Phil

Phil's
drawing of
Dan

THE ONE WORD STORY GA(m)E

P: 'One word story games' are a beautiful way of sharing pure creativity with a friend.

D: You tune into each other's emotional wavelengths to not just finish each other's sentences, but build a story – word by word.

P: Basically, you take it in turns to each say a word and try to tell a story!

D: And what you are left with is often either profound or a horrifying mess. Let's give it a go! I'll say the first word, here we go:

Once day

D: 'Once day' are you kidding me? Oh my god, Phil.

P: I'm sorry! I wasn't thinking, let's just start again.

D: Okay ... here we go. One word each at a time – that makes sense, I'll go first again. Let's make a wonderful story.

Once upon a time in London, a tiny door was discovered underneath a soldier standing next to Buckingham Palace. Behind the tiny door was a giant otter named Gary. Gary's eyes were carrots because he couldn't see after the incident involving angry waiters. Today Gary decided to go into the city to destroy the London Eye. When he got there he released his emotions as he realised he didn't have a friend to play with. Gary died of loneliness.

D: Wow.

P: That was so sad I didn't think the story was going in that direction.

D: I told you it would either be profound or a mess, and that was both.

P: One more! I'll go first this time:

Aliens are secretly watching us poop because unbeknownst to us, they can use our poop as fuel for their probes. The probes are used for working out whether humans can sing or not. The aliens were working for Simon Cowell to discover the next Leona Lewis. When aliens discover this singer, they will absorb their voice and insert it into the Boy Band Generator to take over the minds of young teens across Earth and eat their brains. It will be glorious when they finally sing and the Universe will bow before their sexy coordinated rhythm.

P: That was terrifying.

D: And probably true. I can't decide whether that's a script for a future blockbuster movie or an unearthed conspiracy theory. Better than most of this book that we spent ages thinking about.

P: Either way, that was the one word story game! You can see how it's really fun.

D: Or a terrible mistake.

P: Why not try it with your friends and see what incredible stories you make together! One word at a time.

THE APOCALYPSE

D: Hello and welcome to Going Deep with Dan and Phil.

P: Going deep? Really?

D: You don't even know what the idea of this is yet, so don't shoot it down already, idea-sniper.

P: I'm totally not an idea-sniper. Okay what's your idea?

D: Well we've discussed a wide range of things in this book. People have got to know our early lives, our YouTube stories, what we're like as people – so I thought why not take it to the next level?

P: How do you plan to level us up, Dan? Some kind of mushroom?

D: Nope. By discussing deep and meaningful things. You know those conversations you have with friends at 2am that end with you both going 'woah'. I'd like to share that with our readers!

P: Getting intimate, I like it.

D: Now you're making it strange.

P: Okay, sorry. So what are we talking about first, Deep Daniel?

D: Don't call me that. The Apocalypse!

P: Wow that is deep! Like the movie *Deep Impact*.

D: Yes, Phil, exactly like that. Wow an acceptable pun well done.

P: Thanks, I thought that was good too.

D: So, Phil, how do you think the world is going to end?

P: I think the sun is just going to explode one day without any warning.

D: Well, due to light speed and stuff, we'd have about eight minutes' warning before the many varieties of death come for us.

P: Eight whole minutes. How would you spend them if you saw the sun explode in the sky?

D: Probably make some microwave popcorn, sit in my sofa crease, say goodbye on the internet and listen to some cool apocalypse music.

P: That's a pretty good plan! Plus, when the wave of fire hits us, one of the popcorn kernels you ate might pop inside your melting stomach.

D: Nice and graphic there, Phil. Might have put me off popcorn for a while.

P: So if the sun doesn't randomly explode how do you think our world will end?

D: Well brushing aside the likelihood of humans destroying it themselves, I've always fancied the idea of a giant meteor indiscriminately cruising into earth and obliterating it.

P: Couldn't we just fly up to it and blow it up like Bruce Willis whilst Aerosmith plays in the background.

D: I thought you were a *Deep Impact* man?

P: Only for the puns. *Armageddon* has the key to my heart.

D: Somehow I think the logistics of the meteor-exploding operation would be a bit more complicated than in the movies. I think it's more likely that we'll have the technology to just bail on earth and populate another planet.

P: Where would we go?

D: Mars seems a bit of a depressing dust-fest so I hope they find somewhere more interesting soon.

P: Not everyone could get on the ship though. How would people get chosen to be rescued?

D: I'm guessing you're either important or some kind of lotto?

P: Do you think I'd be important enough to get on?

D: Well, I mean, this is just a hypothetical spaceship and I don't want to make you all depressed, so sure, Phil, you'd totally get on the rocket.

P: Yay!

D: Any other theories? What if it doesn't come from space and the threat lies within our space-bubble?

P: What if nature turns against us? Imagine all the trees suddenly decide they've had enough and reverse drink our oxygen and we all die. The clouds could all rain acid or the ground could open and close like chomping jaws of destruction.

D: I'm not sure how likely that is but I'd sure as hell pay to see that at the cinema.

P: THE NATUREPOCALYPSE

D: Though saying it's unlikely, new strange things are discovered on our planet every day!

P: Like Ligers.

D: I think Ligers are fairly old news but they are pretty cool.

P: I'm all for tiger/lion relationships personally.

D: How progressive of you.

P: I'm also suspicious of ants.

D: Why's that?

P: They're too organised and there's too many of them. They are definitely planning something and could totally take over the world if they wanted!

D: Wow, apparently there are 1,500,000 ants for every human on Earth.

P: See I told you! Antapocalypse! It's the only real theory. I bet it will happen in 57 years.

D: I can't help but feel we got a bit side-tracked and this maybe ended up less deep than I originally intended.

P: You could say we had some good 'bANTer'!

D: See now that totally undid the clever reference you made earlier.

P: Aw really? Hey, can I pick the topic next time? I have a great idea!

D: Well I dunno, this was kind of supposed to be my thing that I have a whole plan for.

P: Pretty please! I promise it'll be so deep you'll get stuck and never be able to climb out.

D: That got weird fast so I'm just going to agree to make it stop. We'll see you next time on Going Deep for another spirited discussion on the fundamental questions of our universe.

PHIL YOUR FUTURE HUSBAND

BECAUSE YOU'RE IT!

Touch

Dan's neck

PEPPERONI NOSE!

I can't quit your wires!

we just get high off the sharpie fumes.

Hey sexy lady let's make out

you are blind

SCREAMING NIPPLES

I'D ACTUALLY PICKLE A PICKLE

EVERYONE JUST UNSUBSCRIBED

WE JUST GET HIGH OFF OF THE SHARPIE FUMES

REASONS WHY DAN'S A FAIL (SO FAR)

LEFTHANDEDISM

It's a cruel affliction so, given the right-handed bias of our society, it should be a crime to force this on young impressionable children. How would you feel if literally everything was backwards or upside down?!

HUMAN INTERACTION

I just don't like talking to people, okay. Yes, I would live on the moon if I had an infinitely stocked fridge and an internet connection.

BUTTERFINGERS

I inexplicably drop things, sometimes. Don't let me hold your newborn or your grandma's ashes.

SPIRALS OF LIES

If I tell a white lie to spare someone's feelings, it will spiral out of control into a ridiculous fairy tale of deceit that will get more and more extreme until it implodes, destroying my social life.

I MUMBLE

You won't be able to understand 99% of the things I say. Even if you have to say 'what?' on the impossibly awkward third time, please tell me if you can't understand me. Just don't bother going to a party with me, I'm effectively mute.

I TALK TO MYSELF

It's pretty weird, I know. I just don't have that bit in my brain to tell me to keep thoughts inside my head and instead they silently come out of my mouth. I think that people avoiding me in busy shops is an advantage personally.

I'M A MESS

I drop things behind furniture to avoid properly sorting them. I hide clothes in a vertical mountain inside my wardrobe. All other missing objects I blame on thieving, stealthy, inter-dimensional goblins. Only rational explanation.

INAPPROPRIATE WINKING

I don't know why I do it but I do. I don't know when it will happen, probably at the worst moments, but I will just randomly bust out a wink. I promise if I ever do it to you, it doesn't mean anything; it's just a horribly, horribly confused impulse I get and nothing more. Please don't contact the authorities.

I CARE TOO MUCH

I'm overly empathetic to the point that I actually annoy my friends at parties with how concerned I am for their enjoyment.

PSYCHO THOUGHTS

I sometimes contemplate my own ability to murder people. IT'S FINE, I WON'T DO IT! I just think about how I could, we all could. The void is calling. It wants me to jump into it.

WEB HISTORY

I'm irrationally paranoid of anyone touching my computer in case they see the horrific secrets of my hard drive. I don't think there's anything bad on there but, come on, who trusts their 3am browsing?

PROCRASTINATION

I suffer from chronic procrastination and would go to extreme lengths that require ironically massive amounts of effort to put off doing something I need to finish.

NEAR-DEATH EXPERIENCES

I'm prone to constantly having near-fatal accidents. It'll never actually happen but I'll get close at least twice a week. Try to stay a metre away from me at all times and keep an eye out for all objects, moving vehicles and limbs. You never know what might happen.

COOL HANDSHAKES

I just don't get them. I'm sorry; I've practised, I've looked at video tutorials, but if you come up to me expecting a weird high-five-shoulder-bump-thing I'll probably just fall over and it'll be embarrassing for both of us.

PERSONAL SPACE

Touch my neck and I will kill you. It's not difficult.

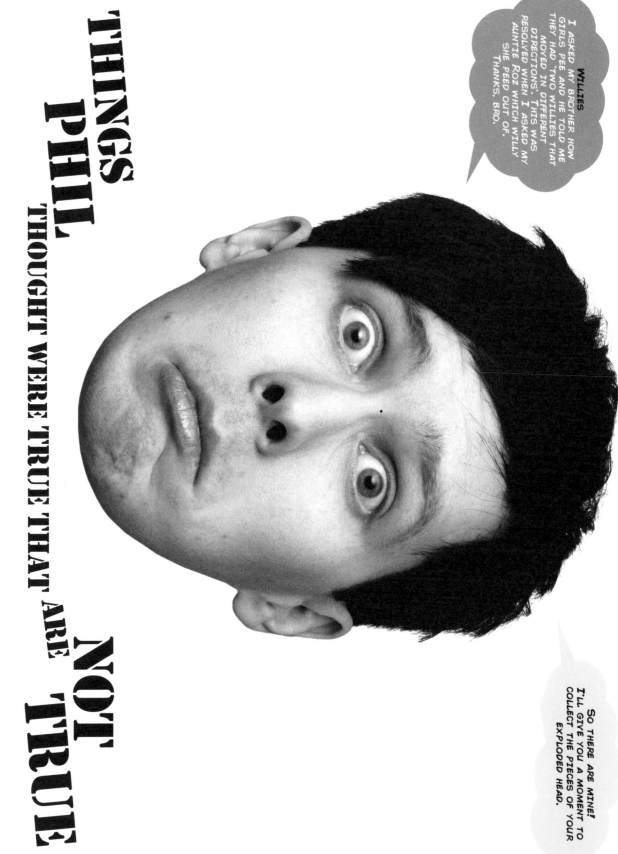

THINGS PHIL THOUGHT WERE TRUE THAT ARE NOT TRUE

WILLIES

I ASKED MY BROTHER HOW GIRLS PEE AND HE TOLD ME THEY HAD TWO WILLIES THAT MOVED IN DIFFERENT DIRECTIONS. THIS WAS RESOLVED WHEN I ASKED MY AUNTIE ROZ WHICH WILLY SHE PEED OUT OF. THANKS, BRO.

SO THERE ARE MINE! I'LL GIVE YOU A MOMENT TO COLLECT THE PIECES OF YOUR EXPLODED HEAD.

THE MOMENT WHEN YOU SUDDENLY DISCOVER THAT YOUR WHOLE LIFE HAS BEEN A LIE. LIKE THE CARPET OR YOUR EXISTENCE HAS BEEN WHIPPED OUT FROM UNDERNEATH YOU AND YOU DOUBT EVERYTHING YOU'VE EVER LEARNED. AKA - WHEN SOMETHING YOU THOUGHT WAS TRUE TURNS OUT NOT TO BE TRUE.

FOR EXAMPLE, AGED 13 WHEN I VISITED AN AQUARIUM AND SAW A SEAHORSE. MY WHOLE LIFE I HAD BELIEVED THEY WERE MYTHICAL CREATURES, BUT THERE WAS ONE JUST HAPPILY FLOATING AROUND IN A TANK. IT COMPLETELY BLEW MY MIND AND I HAVEN'T BEEN THE SAME SINCE. YOU MAY NOT EVEN KNOW HOW MANY OF THE THINGS YOU BELIEVE ARE REALLY LIES SO ON THIS PAGE I WILL NOW LIST ALL OF MINE TO HELP SPREAD THE WORD OF TRUTH.

CATS
I THOUGHT THEY LITERALLY HAD NINE LIVES. THANKFULLY I DIDN'T HAVE A CAT TO TEST THAT THEORY.

BLUE FROM BLUES CLUES
IS A GIRL. SLIGHTLY LESS PEOPLE ARE AFFECTED THAN TWEETIE PIE.

TWEETIE PIE IS A BOY.
THIS CHANGES EVERYTHING.

TONSIL TENNIS
MY FRIEND TOLD ME THAT THE WAY TO KISS A GIRL WAS TO PUT YOUR TONGUE ALL THE WAY INTO THE BACK OF HER THROAT. LET'S JUST SAY MY FIRST KISS DIDN'T END WELL.

BELLY BUTTONS
I THOUGHT THAT BABIES WERE BORN OUT OF WOMEN'S BELLY BUTTONS. DON'T ASK ME WHAT I THOUGHT MINE WAS FOR.

DIDDY KONG
I THOUGHT DIDDY KONG WAS A GIRL.

CHRISTMAS MINCE PIES
FOR MOST OF MY LIFE I THOUGHT THEY CONTAINED ACTUAL BEEF MINCE.

DISNEY LOGO
UNTIL VERY RECENTLY I THOUGHT THE 'D' IN THE DISNEY LOGO WAS SOME KIND OF WEIRD CURLY 'G'. I THOUGHT IT WAS SECRETLY 'GISNEY' BUT NO ONE TALKED ABOUT IT. THEN ONE NIGHT WATCHING ALADDIN ALL OF A SUDDEN I SAW THE D! MIND BLOWING STUFF.

AUSTRALIA
I DID NOT UNDERSTAND HOW PEOPLE COULD BE STANDING ON THE OTHER SIDE OF THE WORLD WITHOUT FALLING OFF INTO SPACE.

MARRIAGE
AT A VERY YOUNG AGE I THOUGHT ALL BOYS WERE DESTINED TO MARRY THEIR MUMS! THANKFULLY I GREW OUT OF THAT ONE PRETTY FAST.

PERIODS
I THOUGHT A PERIOD WAS JUST A HOLIDAY RETREAT FOR WOMEN. IT TURNS OUT IT'S QUITE THE OPPOSITE.

COWS
I THOUGHT MILK WAS COW PEE.

PSYCHIC POWERS
MY BROTHER CONVINCED ME WE ALL HAD PSYCHIC POWERS AND IF I STARED AT A CUP FOR LONG ENOUGH I COULD MOVE IT WITH MY MIND! I SPENT A LONG TIME STARING AT CUPS.

PARACHUTES
FROM VIDEOS OF PEOPLE PARACHUTE JUMPING, I THOUGHT THAT WHEN THE PARACHUTE OPENED PEOPLE WERE SENT HURTLING UPWARDS INTO THE SKY. I THEN HAD IT EXPLAINED THAT IT'S JUST THE PERSON HOLDING THE CAMERA CONTINUING TO FALL.

HOT DOGS
I THOUGHT THEY CONTAINED ACTUAL DOG MEAT. I WAS VERY YOUNG.

SEX
MY GRANDMA TOLD ME THAT SEX WAS A SPECIAL KISS BETWEEN A HUSBAND AND A WIFE. I WORRIED THAT WHEN I GOT OLDER I WOULD GET A GIRL PREGNANT BY KISSING HER THE WRONG WAY.

2009

2010

2011

2012

2013

2014

BEHIND

Danisnotonfire

HELLO AND WELCOME TO OUR SHOW BEHIND THE CAMERA WHERE WE LEARN THE SECRETS BEHIND THE MAGIC OF MAKING VIDEOS. TODAY WE ARE JOINED BY DAN HOWELL, ALSO KNOWN AS 'DANISNOTONFIRE'!

D: Hi there! Thanks for having me on.

SO. DANISNOTONFIRE, WHERE DO YOU SEE ITS PLACE IN THE YOUTUBE WORLD, WHAT'S YOUR ANGLE?

D: I guess I just think of myself as an entertainer. At the end of the day, in whatever form, I make content designed to entertain people. I always try to be creative though!

LET'S TALK ABOUT THAT. YOU'RE NOT REALLY A 'VLOGGER' LIKE OTHERS AND YET YOUR CONTENT IS VERY PERSONALITY LED?

D: Yeah well I think I'm a 'vlogger' in the sense that I make video blog posts. Blog posts about the world, about myself, but they're definitely creations that I think of in terms of writing and performance and editing. Every video is me doing my creative take on something! I'm not really the reality-star kind of vlogger whose content is mainly about following their day-to-day life.

HOW DO YOU COME UP WITH YOUR IDEAS?

D: I never try to think 'what would people want to watch' or 'what would be popular' as then I think it's insincere and hard to make passionately. All of my videos come out of personal inspiration from things I see or happen to me. I just make videos about life – my stories, my opinions – and try to make them fun. I have a 'video ideas' file on my computer with years' worth of ideas in it!

CAN WE HAVE A LOOK?

D: Sure. Each line is an individual video idea I could make tomorrow – no spoilers though!

SO YOU'VE GOT AN IDEA, HOW DOES THAT TURN INTO SOMETHING PEOPLE WATCH?

D: Well once I've got the idea I 'write' it. I don't strictly 'script' videos as then it's a bit unnatural so what I do is bulletpoint what I want to say and write down any great quotes I came up with and then try my best to say it in front of a camera. The tough bit is deciding how I want to creatively interpret the idea. You could do anything in an infinite number of ways. Eventually I just have to settle on something, write it out and then go through it making sure it's perfect.

THE CAMERA

HOW IMPORTANT IS THE VISUAL SIDE OF IT FOR YOU?

D: Well, I think it's good to have a decent camera so people can see you well. I don't really know much about the technical side of filmmaking so I try to do what I can with what I have, which is my camera and my editing. I'm definitely a substance-over-style kind of guy though. For me it's all about the quality of the content and as long as it looks good it's fine!

AND WHAT ABOUT THE EDITING, YOU DON'T HAVE LOTS OF CRAZY EFFECTS BUT IT DOESN'T LOOK LIKE YOU JUST SLAP IT TOGETHER?

D: No! There's two kinds of 'editing'. One is post-production which is things like effects and colours and graphics, but real 'editing' is choosing what to leave in and what to leave out. I honestly believe that editing is an art form and if you're good at it you can turn any pile of rubbish into a beautiful sparkling diamond. I definitely spend way too long on every video making sure it's as good as possible.

HAVE YOU EVER MADE A VIDEO AND NOT UPLOADED IT?

D: Only once. I'm a firm believer that you shouldn't start making something until you've prepared it so well you know it'll be good! I always make sure I have a complete idea of the finished product in my head before I begin. The one time I didn't was 'I'm A Mess' which I tried to make in a time limit and decided to refilm it – that taught me that it's better to take your time and be happy with a video than rush and regret!

DO YOU HAVE A FAVOURITE VIDEO YOU'VE MADE?

D: I think the 'Photo Booth Challenge' is definitely the funniest video I've ever made. Which is super-ironic as it's the dumbest idea ever and was so easy to make. Phil and I were choking with laughter editing it. I'm most proud of my videos like 'College Dropout' and 'The Internet Is Mean' as they are the ones that people tell me had a real profound impact on their lives. For me that's the absolute most important thing! I was very creatively proud of my 'Tour of Dan's Brain' video as it was so difficult.

FINALLY, CAN YOU SHOW US WHAT IS BEHIND THE CAMERA?

D: Now this is a spoiler! Immersion ruined.

Danisnotonfire `Video` Trivia

👍 'Danisnotonfire' was my MySpace name when I was 13. There is no meaning behind it, I was going through my 'random phase'.

👍 Before I uploaded 'Hello Internet', there was a video on my channel of me playing a hater message I got sent on Xbox Live after annihilating someone at Halo 3.

👍 I have had three videos removed by YouTube for being 'sexually inappropriate'.

👍 My parents didn't find out about my YouTube channel until someone told my mum at work that I was on the homepage.

👍 For three years my tripod was the camera balanced on a pile of books and DVDs.

👍 Many people think Phil was the man in the suit in my 'How To Use A Gimp' video. It was actually a man I had never met who is usually a TV extra.

👍 For 'DAN IS ON FIRE' I had to hire a 'Film Fire Specialist' to safely immolate me. I wore a special rubber suit underneath my clothes to protect me from the fire but was told 'if you inhale, the fire will go in your lungs and boil you internally'.

👍 I had to delete my 'PSYCHO FRENCH TEACHER' video as the actual French teacher sent YouTube a letter threatening to sue me.

👍 The reason I had curly hair in the scene at Charlie McDonnell's house in 'I Will Go Down With This Ship' is I was so terrified of meeting him I was nervously sweating.

👍 Rhett and Link have asked for the 'Iron Lung' trophy I won for SuperNote 2012 to be sent back to them for several years but I don't know how to mail something so heavy internationally.

👍 Right before filming 'How To Speak INTERNET' with Jack and Finn Harries, Finn accidentally broke the leg of his desk causing everything (including a fish bowl) to smash on the floor. This also cut my arm open which is why I'm wearing a plaster in the video.

👍 I filmed 'I'M A MESS' three months before I uploaded it. For the first time ever I wasn't entirely happy with a video I'd made so I put it on hold until I felt like coming back and improving it.

👍 'THE PANIC ALARM' and 'THE POWER NAP' were originally going to be one video about stupid things I did at work, but I decided to split them into two because I felt they were so good. I also accidentally initially uploaded 'THE POWER NAP' to my side channel danisnotinteresting.

👍 I wanted to direct my Lion vs. Dinosaur 'EXTINCTION RACE' video but couldn't be told half the things that would happen as it had to be a surprise, so I had to blindly trust my friends Ciaran and PJ.

👍 Tyler Oakley and I actually filmed a third video together in case we thought it'd be a bad idea to upload the one we filmed for his channel. He decided to upload it anyway.

👍 After uploading '12 Year Old Dan's Website' the website got so much traffic that the account running it was deleted for going ridiculously over its allowed bandwidth.

👍 'A Tour of Dan's Brain' was the longest I've ever spent on a video as I had to go on multiple odysseys around London to craft the brain and I made a huge mistake. The video worked by putting a green screen underneath the cardboard flaps of the brain, but I accidentally made parts of the design of my brain the same shade of green so I had to do everything twice. Doh.

👍 'Sexy Internet Dating' was removed by YouTube as a guy who we caught trying to catfish people filed a privacy complaint.

👍 I filmed 'The Truth About December' on holiday with my family in India because I had the idea two hours before I had to leave for the airport and ran out of time to film it at home.

👍 I once asked Delia Smith's management if we could collaborate on a cooking video but she turned me down.

> thank you for your request to Delia.
> Dan's channel is lots of fun.
> Delia has had a full on year with the launch of the online cookery school, NCFC, and Delia's Cakes and is now taking a well-earned break. Therefore, I am sorry it is not possible to help with Dan's Christmas Dinner idea.
> Do hope he's enjoying our new Sausage Rolls video on the online cookery school.
>
> Please do thank Dan for his wonderful support for Delia and her recipes.
>
> All best wishes
>
> ███████
>
> ████████████
>
> **Personal Manager to Delia**

BEHIND

AmazingPhil

IN THIS WEEK'S EDITION OF BEHIND THE CAMERA WE HAVE PHIL LESTER, ALSO KNOWN AS 'AMAZINGPHIL'!

P: Thanks for having me.

YOU ASKED US TO PROVIDE 17 RED SKITTLES, A SMALL PUPPY AND A VIOLIN IN YOUR DRESSING ROOM: ANY REASON BEHIND THAT?

P: Well red is the best flavour of sweet, my parents never let me have a puppy so I figured this was my chance, plus my virtual son Dil Howlter is learning violin so I thought I'd encourage him by learning it too.

LET'S HAVE A LOOK AT YOUR CREATIVE PROCESS. WHERE DO YOU GET YOUR IDEAS?

P: I have a lot of video ideas in the shower! I think it's something about completely switching off your mind in a nice warm environment that sparks off a load of weird thoughts. I get most of my ideas from real-life situations, I am a magnet for strange and unusual people. When I met Dan he thought I was making it all up until he witnessed loads of the encounters himself!

DID YOU HAVE ANY WEIRD THOUGHTS IN THE SHOWER THIS MORNING?

P: I have an idea buzzing around my head about using time travel in a video, like a message to my former self. I'm not sure if it'll turn into anything but it's in my ideas book!

YOU HAVE AN IDEAS BOOK? CAN WE SNEAK A PEEK?

P: As you asked nicely here's a little page:

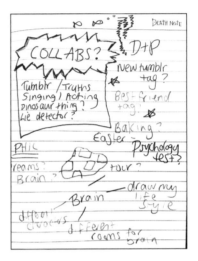

IS FILMING A VLOG AN EASY PROCESS?

P: I wouldn't call it easy! Some days I feel like my tongue is too big for my mouth and it takes me about 17 attempts to say a sentence. The easiness totally depends on the video! Usually I'm fine just rambling about my life but more complicated videos like the tour of my brain can be a bit more of a headache (pun unintended). Still a fun headache to be having though! The easiest videos are collab videos as that's just capturing natural fun with another human.

YOUR EDITING STYLE IS QUITE CREATIVE AND INDIVIDUAL, HOW DID IT COME ABOUT?

P: It's something I've developed over time. I like my videos to all have a similar vibe and I try and think about what would make me smile if I was watching it myself. I like to be able to laugh at myself too, so if I do something really weird with my face I'll happily zoom in and play it back in slow motion.

THE CAMERA

HOW LONG DOES A VIDEO TAKE TO EDIT?

P: It varies a lot! A typical 'Phil vlog' can take me around five hours to edit! I'm very picky so it takes me ages to whittle it down before I'm happy with it.

YOU ALWAYS SEEM SO POSITIVE ON YOUR CHANNEL. DO YOU EVER HAVE BAD DAYS?

P: I am human and I do have my bad days, but I wouldn't make a video about it. I see my channel as something that's hopefully going to improve someone's day! YouTube is a lot of people's nice fun escape from life so I want to make my channel as enjoyable as possible. If I'm having a terrible week I'll just switch off the camera and come back to it when I'm feeling recharged and happy!

WHAT DID YOUR PARENTS THINK ABOUT YOU STARTING YOUTUBE AS A CAREER?

P: Thankfully they've always been incredibly supportive. When I was living at home and had about 10,000 subscribers it still wasn't much of a job, but I told my parents I was really passionate about it and they agreed that I should give it a year and see how it goes. Best decision ever!

NOT ONLY DO YOU HAVE A BA IN ENGLISH LANGUAGE AND LINGUISTICS BUT YOU ALSO HAVE AN MA IN POST-PRODUCTION. THAT'S QUITE IMPRESSIVE.

P: I mean no one wants to brag about academic achievements but I did try really hard with my MA and it helped out with my channel a lot too. I spent an entire summer in a dark editing suite doing my dissertation. I don't think I've ever been so pale.

ARE THERE ANY VIDEOS YOU HAVEN'T BEEN HAPPY WITH?

P: I made a video called 'Dogalikes' which seemed like an awesome idea at the time but it turns out comparing YouTubers to dogs wasn't the greatest idea I've had, which is fine. I unlisted that one pretty quickly.

WHAT'S YOUR FAVOURITE VIDEO YOU HAVE MADE?

P: The 'Punk Edits in Real Life' was really fun to make. I also pranked my mum by telling her I actually got the giant neck tattoo. Another video I loved making is the Tumblr tag video with Dan, it's so nice to see how creative (and mildly disturbing) our audience is.

FINALLY, PHIL, CAN YOU SHOW US WHAT IS BEHIND THE CAMERA?

P: Here you go! A white wall and a camera. No giant film crew or spaceship, unfortunately.

AmazingPhil Video Trivia

👍 Original ideas for my channel name were BuffyPhil, LionPhil, Phil666, FantasticPhil, PHILWORLD and Phil3000.

👍 My lion was in one of the first fan mail packages I ever opened and came from Japan!

👍 I almost deleted the entire channel after getting a hate comment on one video. So glad I didn't.

👍 I didn't tell my friends I made YouTube videos until they all saw me featured on the front page! That was a weird conversation to have.

👍 For three years my 'Tripod' was a camera stacked on a selection of books and DVDs.

👍 I have over 100 private videos! Mainly because they make me cringe so much I don't want millions of people to watch them. Here's some of the thumbnails:

👍 'Phil is Not on Fire 5' had an unseen 20 minutes of footage which was lost when I dropped the SD card in a glass of milk.

👍 In 2008 I made a video called 'The Truth' where I pretended to be an American called Kyle and joked that I had invented the 'Phil character' as I thought British people were cool. It turned out my accent was too convincing as loads of people believed me! I never did post an explanation so sorry to anyone who still thinks I'm a secret American.

👍 We were going to refilm the green velvet cake Halloween baking video with a new recipe after they turned out to be swampy brown cakes, but we thought the footage was too funny not to use!

👍 1% of my audience is age 65+! I hope they draw whiskers on their faces.

Patrick is Dead. 3:57 · 41,449 views · 6 years ago	**The Cube** 2:23 · 37,199 views · 6 years ago	**Reality Test** 1:02 · 21,942 views · 6 years ago	**My Confession** 3:42 · 28,523 views · 6 years ago	**Sunshine** 2:18 · 46,927 views · 6 years ago
Sock Perfection 0:39 · 39,983 views · 6 years ago	**The Silver Button** 2:32 · 90,166 views · 6 years ago	**The Magic Box of Mystery** 3:31 · 26,480 views · 6 years ago	**Musical Socks** 3:31 · 39,054 views · 6 years ago	**AmericanPhil** 0:39 · 111,833 views · 6 years ago
Extreme Weather?!! 3:30 · 18,489 views · 6 years ago	**Goodbye England** 3:16 · 24,836 views · 6 years ago	**Time Travel** 2:44 · 24,210 views · 6 years ago	**The Wish** 2:00 · 94,826 views · 6 years ago	**Super Fun Drawing Game** 4:10 · 56,660 views · 7 years ago
20 Days 2:07 · 38,385 views · 7 years ago	**RoboTube** 8:45 · 40,822 views · 7 years ago	**Mr. Phil built an Ark** 3:03 · 88,264 views · 6 years ago	**DANGER!** 2:39 · 163,014 views · 6 years ago	**Super Mega Number Man** 3:38 · 16,761 views · 7 years ago

👍 140,855 128 👎

👍 I made the 'Toilet Tag' video after dreaming it became the next huge craze on YouTube. Thanks for that one, brain. At least The 7 Second Challenge happened!

👍 I discovered my videos are frequently viewed on a forum for people with sneeze fetishes! They slow down my sneezes and talk about what I may be allergic to. Not creepy at all.

👍 I never planned for 'Draw Phil Naked' to be a thing! I showed one someone sent me in a video then loads of people just started joining in.

👍 Things on my failed list of ideas include 'Changing Colour T-shirt Dance', 'Vlog About Whales' and '100 Thoughts I Have Had Today'.

👍 Here is where I'm the most popular!

Top locations by views
United States
United Kingdom
Canada
Australia
Germany
Sweden
Ireland
New Zealand
Netherlands
Singapore

👍 129 👎 45

Guide to Being a YouTuber

P: One of the things we are always asked the most is advice on being a YouTuber. So many people out there want to try making videos themselves but have no idea where to start, so I thought we had to answer this in our book! Dan isn't convinced this is a good idea.

D: I'm just saying – we're making this book for people to remember our world far into the future and YouTube probably won't exist then. 'Google' will just be known as the all-powerful A.I. that controls and farms humanity as a resource in the inevitable post-singularity future.

P: Well how's about as well as helping the people alive now with interesting advice, we can think of it as a way to preserve our video-making advice for history?

D: That sounds more like it. Maybe this page will be framed in the future 'strange extinct intelligent species and what they did with their spare time' exhibition at the robot museum.

P: Okay, Dan. So here's our combined wisdom and advice on the world of YouTube!

WHY?

The first question is why do you want to do this? To be creative? To share your life with the world? To make new friends? To show off your microwave juggling skills? Think about what's motivating you to make videos. It's always better if people have a genuine motivation behind wanting to be on YouTube other than just 'being famous'!

WHAT?

What kind of videos do you want to make? It's completely up to you! Are you a filmmaker? A comedian? A vlogger? A gamer? A chef?! Think about what you are passionate about and what you can offer to the world. Remember it's okay to be inspired by others but it's not cool to copy! Think about what you like about various YouTubers and why, then try to create something original with your individual spin on it!

IN THE BEGINNING

An introduction is always a great first video! Dive straight into the kind of videos you are going to make on the channel and who you are. Maybe try doing it in a fun and different way that would get people talking about it? Of course you can always use our super-convenient 'YouTube Video Idea Generator' after this!

NAMING THE CHANNEL!

This isn't going to be easy as every human on earth and their grandma has a YouTube account by now, so stumbling across a great name that isn't already taken is like stumbling across a shiny Pokémon.

👍 140,855 132 👎

YES 👍

👍 **MAKE IT MEMORABLE!**
You want a name that sticks in the head of your viewer. Using your actual name can work well! (DanHowell works a lot better than xXGlitterDolphin14714.) It's also an instant introduction and makes you seem more real. Careful what you do if you use your real name though!

👍 **CHOOSE SOMETHING EASY-TO-SPELL**
If someone hears about your channel by word of mouth it has to be easy to spell! 'SeReNdiPitOuSlySUSAN' may do less well than 'SuperSusan'.

👍 **CHOOSE SOMETHING RELATED TO THE CHANNEL**
It's always great to have the vibe of a channel in a username! For example, a gaming channel could use gaming-related words.

NO 👎

👎 **NUMBERS**
Try not to include numbers! Loads of numbers in a username can look a bit distracting and robot like! We'd rather subscribe to LizardPlanet rather than 00Lizard17449875.

👎 **SIMILAR NAMES**
Don't make a channel name too similar to another YouTuber! (Unless you're creating a fan account.) MooDiePie might not do as well as an original name and people might think you are a copycat (or a copydog).

👎 **THINGS YOU MIGHT REGRET LATER**
It might be fine now, but always think about the future! For example if your YouTube channel explodes to 18 billion subscribers overnight and you're called 'Pepsi23' it might be an issue!

EQUIPMENT

Camera: These days most phones or digital cameras are more than good enough for vlogging. Don't feel like you need a fancy DSLR or TV camera right from the start. When it comes to videos, the quality of the content is more important than the camera!

Sound: People being able to hear you well is important. Try to record in a quiet room and make sure whatever microphone you use doesn't make things sound like they are underwater. We always recommend doing tests before properly filming things.

Lighting: You don't need anything super fancy for this either! Usually a bright sunlit room will be fine. Just make sure the window isn't behind you or you'll look like an angel beaming into the room from heaven. If there's no sun you can D.I.Y. by pointing a bright lamp at the wall behind the camera.

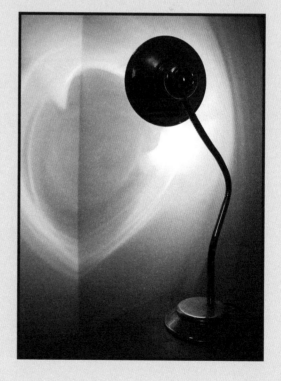

👍 133 👎 45

LOCATION

This depends on what videos you want to make, but for vloggers bedrooms and living rooms are great as they are intimate and feel like you're inviting the audience into your world. You can turn any space into a cool filming zone with objects that reflect your style and personality.

PROPS

Make sure you have everything you need before you start filming. There's nothing worse than getting halfway through a video and realising you have no black pen to draw whiskers on yourself, or red wine to drink while giving advice, or a giant piece of cardboard for your brain.

PLAN AHEAD

We don't recommend just turning on the camera and rambling. For some people it works out great, the rest of the time it's seven minutes of 'why?'. Don't start filming until you've gone over the whole thing in your head so you're ready to go!

FILMING

It's time to film! We're not going to lie, talking to yourself alone in your bedroom is a bit weird. If you do have any housemates or parents either wait until you're home alone or explain to them what you are doing in advance so you can feel confident. Setting up a camera pointing at your bed may confuse a lot of parents so it's probably best to warn them before you start doing it.

At first it might feel strange talking to no one, so imagine you are talking to a friend and you'll come across natural to the audience! Try to be enthusiastic so you command people's attention.

The first 20 seconds or so are the most important so be energetic and to the point so you draw your audience in!

👍 135 👎 45

Here's some good and bad examples of first lines of a video:

'Hi! You will never believe what happened yesterday, I was stalked by a seagull.'

👍 YES. Straight to the point!

'Hi I'm not really sure what to say but I thought I'd just turn on the camera and see how this goes, sorry it's been a while.'

👎 NO. This makes you sound like you don't have any clear reason for making a video and isn't very engaging. Also never waste time apologising for late videos or similar things, just do it instead!

EDITING

Editing sounds complicated and scary but it doesn't have to be! All you're doing is sticking the good bits of something together and adding things to it.

You don't need a fancy expensive program, most computers come with free editing software that's perfectly fine for beginners. If you're ever confused, look up a YouTube tutorial! There are thousands of videos teaching you how to do absolutely everything.

For vlogs we recommend editing out all the 'um's and 'ah's to make it snappy and find some music to make it nice to listen to (not Britney Spears though or you'll be smited by the copyright bot).

When we've finished editing we always show our videos to our friends for any feedback as it's really useful to hear other people's perspectives.

TITLE

Short and snappy titles are usually best, though if you've seen our bible-length DanAndPhilGAMES titles you'll know that we don't always follow that rule. Try and think of something related to the video that will make people curious enough to click on it! 'SEAGULL STALKER' would sound much more exciting than 'My Holiday in France'. Try not to be too cheesy or clickbaity though!

THUMBNAIL

Choose a nice clear close-up of yourself talking, or a key point of the video that makes it look like something you want to see moving!

UPLOADING

It's best to upload in the evenings as more people will be hanging out on their computers rather than being at school or work or asleep!

WHY IS NOBODY WATCHING?

Ok great I've made a video and it's up. How do I get someone to watch it?

Unfortunately there is no magic formula to getting subscribers (unless Pewdiepie is secretly a genie). Here are some tips:

Make friends in the community! You might be lost in the comments on a huge YouTuber's video, but there's always people starting out on YouTube looking for friends. Comment on their videos and collaborate with people you like! Don't advertise yourself by spamming people's comments though. If your content's good people will notice. Integrity is important.

Use social media! Get on Facebook, Twitter, Tumblr and other accounts that people use to share their favourite clips. You can share your videos with your friends and family and if you have a place for your audience to follow you they can share and support your content too.

Stick at it! It took over a year for the AmazingPhil channel to get over 100 subscribers. Most successful YouTubers made videos for years with nobody watching just because they loved it. If you're doing it because you enjoy it then it shouldn't matter how many people watch — even if you get 100 views on a video that's 100 people whose days you have improved!

There's so much we could say about this that it could fit in its own book but we hope any budding YouTubers out there found this helpful. Good luck!

👍 137 👎 45

YOUTUBE ▶ VIDEO IDEA GENERATOR

D: We all know creativity can be hard. Especially when starting out! You have a camera, your brain and the infinite possibilities of the universe. What do you make a video about?!

P: The question I get asked the most is 'I want to be a YouTuber, what should my first video be about?' so we created this handy YouTube video idea generator.

D: Yep. Why put yourself through the stress of being original, when you can throw a bunch of things that already exist together to make something 'new'!

We take no responsibility for any incidents that occur as a result of this page.

FIRST CHOOSE YOUR BIRTH MONTH

JANUARY:	VLOG ABOUT
FEBRUARY:	BLINDFOLDED DRAW
MARCH:	PERFORM A SONG ABOUT
APRIL:	CREATE AN ARTISTIC FILM ABOUT
MAY:	MAKE A COSTUME OF
JUNE:	RANT FOR ONE MINUTE ABOUT
JULY:	PRANK SOMEONE USING
AUGUST:	DO AN INTERPRETIVE DANCE ABOUT
SEPTEMBER:	DO A BEAUTY TUTORIAL ON HOW TO LOOK LIKE
OCTOBER:	MAKE A MUSIC VIDEO ABOUT
NOVEMBER:	HAVE A RAP BATTLE AGAINST
DECEMBER:	CREATE A LIFE-SIZE PLASTICINE STOP MOTION FILM OF

NOW CHOOSE YOUR BIRTH DATE!

1. A WARTHOG
2. A CACTUS
3. LIZARDS
4. AN OCTOPUS
5. GODZILLA
6. A HOUSE PLANT
7. YOUR MUM
8. A GOOSE
9. THE EIFFEL TOWER
10. YOUR FAVOURITE EMOJI
11. BEES
12. PHIL'S EAR
13. AN OLD LADY CALLED DOROTHY
14. AN EAR HAIR
15. A SPOON
16. A NARWHAL
17. BACON
18. A SOCK
19. A SLICE OF BEEF
20. DEATH
21. BUTTS
22. UNICORNS
23. THE END OF THE WORLD
24. A TINY SEAL
25. YOUR PET
26. THE PLANET JUPITER
27. A SPECK OF DUST
28. A LLAMA
29. A LION
30. PANCAKES
31. YOUR GREATEST FEAR

Congratulations!
And there's your first video.

P: Okay let's test it out on Dan. When's your birthday?

D: Seriously, you don't know my birthday?

P: Oh. 11 June! So, Dan ... rant for one minute about bees!

D: Sounds like a winner right there. What about you?

P: 30 January ... vlog about pancakes!

D: Haven't you already done that like nine times?

P: See, it generates great video ideas!

D: Fine, but if your birthday is 21 September you might want to keep that one private.

P: We look forward to watching all the incredible videos this generator will create.

National Rail
Britain's train companies working together

nanoblock

...and Piano
...ンドピアノ
...150 pieces

oyster
2012 Transport for London

To
LONDON TERMINALS
From
READING STATIONS FGW FIRSTGROUP
Route
Valid until 15-MCH-15
Start Date 15-MCH-15
Ticket Type FGW WEEKEND UPG
Class 1ST 1ST
Number 02277 596...
Adult ONE
Child NIL
...14 616375

NOSE WORKOUT

I'D TELL YOU, BUT WE'D HAVE TO KILL YOU

ola

PHIL, DO THE SEXY ENDSCREEN DANCE

Can you explain the theory behind the whiskers?

Shhhhhhhhhack

TACO

CLAWS

SHOULDER BOOBS

RICKY BLITZ

I LOOK LIKE A SERIAL KILLER

OLÉ

Dinosaura

CAP

Danny, it's time for your neck exam

FinGernaiLs For Nipples

IT'S SO SQUEAKY AND CHAFING

DRAGONS

Shhhhhhhhhack

DANINATOR

skin coat

GOAT

The Emojinterview

>>>>>>>>>>>>>>>>>>>>>>>>>>

Answer only using emojis!

How are you?

D: ☕😎✌️

P: 😬👌

Most recently used emojis?

D: 👦✨❄️🎄😱🎁👲😉😃😹😄😍😔✈️🔲🛀🌞😸😈🐲📍🚋🚃😀🎉🔃

P: 😬⭐🐢⭐😬🎈❗📦😆🐴❓😔💃🚀😳🔥💀👍❄️😮😟😕✨🐺

Find an emoji you have never used

D: 👡

P: 🚥

Favourite emoji?

D: 👽

P: 🐗

What was the first thing you did when you woke up?

D: ❄️👦❄️👙👕👖🔥👍

P: ☕

Describe your dream last night

D: 👹😱🏃👺🎷🚶💢💀👦🎉

P: 🐙🐙🏢🔥😱🏃🐙😨🐙👅💀

What does your ideal Saturday evening consist of?

D: 😔➡️🍕➡️😬➡️🍕🍕🍕➡️💀

P: 🎥🍕

What is the last thing you will see before you die?

D: 💥🔫🐴🔜

P: 👽

What will you be doing in twenty years?

D: 🍦😭🎮💭💸💸

P: 👴💬📹

What does the future
look like?

D: 🙇🙏🗿✨☁️☁️👽👋

P: 🌊🐙👑

What is your worst
nightmare?

D: 🔥💻🔥

P: 🐴🔪

What would you buy with
£10 million?

D: 🚀💎🍪🍫🍩

P: 📊

What is your first memory?

D: 💫💦😷👶

P: 👟

What do you do on a plane?

D: 😐🍸❓📺

P: 👓📖

Dream holiday?

D: 🚶😴🏂🍵📖

P: 🇯🇵

What has writing this book
been like?

D: 😁💭❗✏️😂

P: 😆

Phil. Describe Dan in
4 emojis

P: 👾🍵💭🎶

Dan. Describe Phil in
4 emojis

D: 🧔🐗🌟👾

Goodbye!

D: 👋👦💯

P: 😴

145

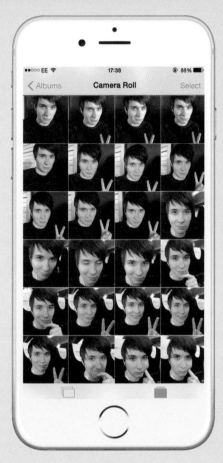

Unsuccessful Selfies: Dan

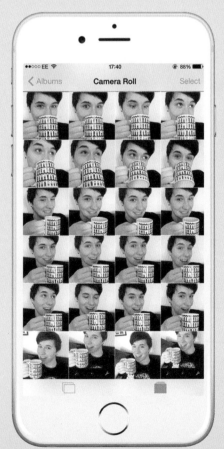
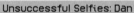

Unsuccessful Selfies: Phil

PLAYER 3 DIL

NAME:
DIL

INTERNET NAME:
DIL JAMECHAL HOWLTER

HEIGHT:
6FT 2"

FAVOURITE COLOUR:
CLOWN-PYJAMA GREEN

ANIMAL OF CHOICE:
JONATHAN THE MINNOW

WEAKNESS:
DELICATE CROCKERY

SPECIAL POWER:
SURVIVING MULTIPLE
ELECTROCUTIONS

QUOTE:
BENZI CHIBNA LOOBLE
BAZEBNI GWEB

DRAW DIL'S LIFE

Sul Sul! Kai bar Dil tu bay su drawm mo lifzar

Oh foo lar kobar Dan zi Phil tay

Lum kobar say Sims refuntay

Oh sar kobar zum scrumutar zi caratu creazomar

Heru zum bar botar namutay

Say sratzo raznay parl

Oh far townutay ko Oasislar Springs

Oh me hava lawnmug

Tay lawnuzy Owl sliduzar

Oh sar dreamizil zu mixobar busa luzee

Desar sum favlor poseratarl

Zum day jadosi um simoleons tar

151

BEHIND

DanAndPhilGames

SO WHY A GAMING CHANNEL?

D: Basically? We spent all our free time when we weren't making danisnotonfire and AmazingPhil videos playing video games, so we thought 'why not just film it and put it on the internet'!

P: It's something we had both talked about individually for ages!

D: Yeah, literally. I have a file on my computer from 2012 where I was about to make one:

> gaming channel - danisnotonline?
> think gaming shows
> let's play's
> research what kind of categories there are for gaming channels
> whatever's top of the charts
> old school games
> hardes ps1 platforming moments
> scariest ps1 moments
> gw2
> whatever's trendy
>
> mason's why don't a fail
>
> youtube plans
>
> rich text (RTF) - 1 KB
> Created Wednesday, 23 May 2012 16:31

WHY DIDN'T YOU?

D: Mainly because of Radio 1 and we were moving to London. We thought we'd 'settle into London life' and see how things are going before starting a big new thing – turns out settling in took a year and a half!

SO WHY A JOINT GAMING CHANNEL?

P: Mainly because if we were both invested in it we couldn't procrastinate away from it individually. We figured we would feature in each other's so often we might as well do it together! Plus our audience loves videos twice as much if it's a 'Dan and Phil' thing.

WAS IT ALWAYS GOING TO BE CALLED DANANDPHILGAMES?

P: We settled on that in the end as it's basically just the best name, but we had some alternatives! I just found the file of our brainstorm:

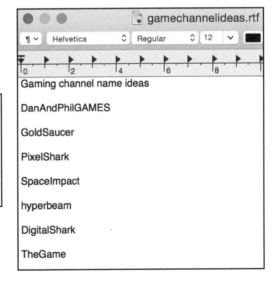

gamechannelideas.rtf

Gaming channel name ideas

DanAndPhilGAMES

GoldSaucer

PixelShark

SpaceImpact

hyperbeam

DigitalShark

TheGame

D: I'm kind of sad we didn't call it 'TheGame'.

P: Thankfully for the rest of the internet it was already taken!

HOW DO YOU DECIDE WHAT GAMES TO PLAY?

D: We decided from the start to play games that we love. A lot of people just go with whatever's trendiest at the time because people will be searching for it and that gets views. We wanted to convince people we were passionate about gaming though by playing our favourites!

THE CAMERA

YOU PICK A LOT OF THINGS YOU'VE NEVER PLAYED BEFORE THOUGH?

P: I think there's a magic to playing something for the first time so everyone can laugh at how bad you are. I always find it really interesting and fun to see someone new reacting to something that I'm really familiar with!

HOW IS IT DIFFERENT TO FILMING YOUR OTHER VIDEOS?

D: Well, for one, we don't really have to come up with totally new ideas every time. We just film us playing and having lols and edit it into a video! The lack of creative pressure makes it very fun.

P: You need a whole other set of technology too. The process of capturing video game footage and editing it is very complicated!

D: I let Phil do all that. I tried to research it once and my brain nearly started dribbling out of my ear. I just look after the cables so they don't turn into a big black wiry ball of hell.

WHAT'S THE SECRET TO GOOD GAMING VIDEOS?

D: Lots of people make lots of different kinds of gaming content. It's as diverse as comedy or vlogging. You could do reviews, or videos about gaming culture and the industry, 'machinima' and then there's of course 'Let's Plays'.

P: We're definitely a 'Let's Play' channel! I think the magic behind those is it's like you're just hanging out with people you find entertaining. It's like any sort of sport or news comedy show that reacts to things that are happening – we just joke around and react to the game as a mutual interest to talk about.

D: I think you can still be a bit creative though, especially getting your personality through in the editing. I mean, this channel was supposed to be our super easy 'film it and whack it together' project but I ended up spending ages editing these ones too! I genuinely think all of our gaming videos are hilarious and I watch them back at least three times after uploading them. I think it just says a lot about our chemistry!

FINALLY, WHY DO YOU THINK THE LIFE OF YOUR SIM 'DIL HOWLTER' IS SUCH A SUCCESS?

D: People just like to watch other people playing house.

P: Yes I think the idea of Dan and Phil having a son and building a home, even though that's not at all what it is, appeals to a lot of people.

D: It's nice and domestic. For real, though, we had no idea how funny and amazing it would be. It's really like he's a real special little guy with his own personality. Wait, do you reckon he might be dead when the person is reading this book?

P: Don't say those things, Dan! I will hack the game if I have to to make him immortal. At the time of writing he is alive and well, just like he will be forever in all of our hearts.

BRAIN FARTS

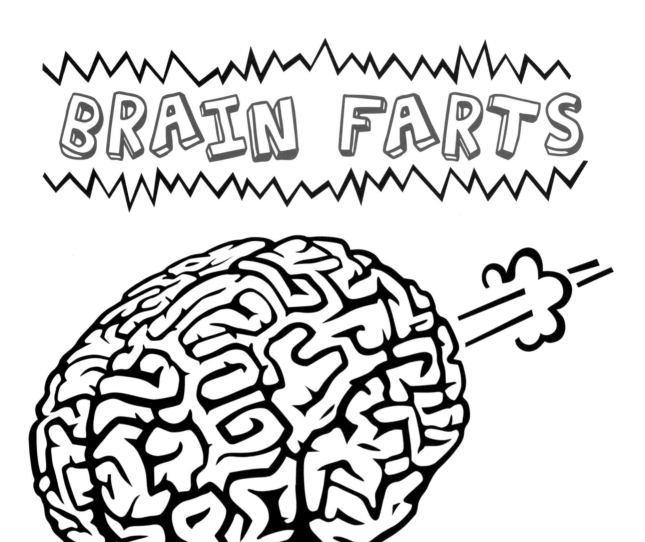

A 'BRAIN FART' IS WHEN YOU WRITE OUT THE FIRST THING THAT COMES INTO YOUR HEAD WITH NO FILTER. START WITH ANY WORD AND INSTANTLY PUT DOWN WHATEVER YOU THINK OF NEXT – IT PROBABLY WON'T MAKE ANY SENSE, BUT THAT'S THE POINT. PURE, UNCENSORED BRAIN-WAFFLE. WE DECIDED TO DO JUST THAT ON THESE PAGES. PLEASE DON'T PSYCHOANALYSE ANY OF THIS.

PHIL

THE MICE WERE SCREAMING AS TINY BADGERS WERE TURNING INTO METEORS WHICH LANDED IN THE LAKE WHERE LIFE BEGAN. THE COASTER IS MADE OUT OF TIN FOIL WHICH DOESN'T HEAT THE MUG OF WARM SOUP THAT IS FILLED WITH WORMS ON HALLOWEEN WHERE PANDA MASKS ARE ALL THE RAGE. TEETH ARE SHARP AND BLOOD IS POURING OUT OF THE WATERFALL WHICH ISN'T VERY CHRISTMASSY HOPEFULLY I WON'T GET DENTAL FLOSS IN MY STOCKING THIS YEAR WHY ARE THEY EVEN CALLED STOCKINGS WHAT IS THAT REFLECTION IN MY GLASSES IT LOOKS LIKE THE BUTT OF AN ANGEL WHO WAS BETTER OR WORSE THAN SPIKE I THINK I LIKED SPIKE WHICH MAKES ME WANT TO TWIST MY HAIR INTO A UNICORN HORN. SHOULD I GET MY MUM THE UNICORN SLIPPERS OR THE HEATED NARWHAL SLIPPERS WHEN THEY COME IN STOCK BUT SHIPPING IS EXPENSIVE FROM THE US DO THEY EVEN COME ON A SHIP? DID BIGFOOT HAVE LARGE CLAWS OR FEET LIKE A CAT? THEY PURR BUT WHAT DOES THE SOUND COME FROM IS IT LIKE THE NOISE WHEN A DONKEY IS LAUGHING OUTSIDE MY GRANDMA'S HOUSE EVERY MORNING? I WONDER IF THAT DONKEY AFFECTED THE PROPERTY MARKET MONOPOLY I WANT TO PLAY BUT NO ONE LIKES IT AS MUCH AS ME. I THINK I SHOULD STOP NOW.

DAN

IN THE BEGINNING THERE WAS A DAN. A DAN WITH THE PLAN, HE WAS THE MAN WITH A HAND THAT COULD REACH UP INTO THE SKY AND PULL DOWN ANYTHING HE WANTED, SO ONE DAY HE WENT TO A SHOP AND YELLED OUT 'WHY WOULD YOU DO THIS TO ME I DON'T UNDERSTAND FOR GOD'S SAKE WHERE ARE MY SHOES WHO DID YOU TAKE THEM FROM?' IT STARTED RAINING AND THE DOGS HOWLED A FINAL SWAN SONG OF JUSTICE INTO THE COLD NIGHT. THE WEEPING TREES SWAYED IN THE WIND OF FORGETFULNESS AS THE WORLD PLUMMETED INTO A DARKNESS ONLY KNOWN TO THOSE WHO HAVE THE SECRETS. I REMEMBER LAST TUESDAY LIKE IT WAS MY LAST WITH THE BACON ON SALE AND THE FIERY HATS IN THE DISPLAY OF THE NEW SHOP WINDOW. 'WHO ARE YOU TO SAY THESE THINGS TO ME?' I CAST TO MY SHADOW AS IT RAN AWAY FOR NOT ACCEPTING THE TRUTH. WILL WE EVER HAVE THE ANSWERS? KICKING THINGS IS ILLEGAL YOU SHOULD KNOW THAT BY NOW. IT'S BEEN A COLD DARK CAVE AND A FIERY WONDERFUL 400 YEARS ON THIS PLANET AND THE FINAL LESSON AT THE END OF THE DAY IS NOT WHICH SOCKS DON'T MATCH UP IN PAIRS, BUT WHICH UMBRELLA YOU TAKE ON HOLIDAY TO A SANDY BEACH. BAZINGA.

DAN'S FEARS

Why are we doing this? I mean we're literally writing out all of our weaknesses ready to be exploited by an evil genius/future dystopian government.

THE SUPERNATURAL

Poltergeists, witches, demons – you name it, if it's a magically powered evil being that defies the rules of reality, I'm terrified of it. Which is funny because I do not believe that any of these things exist. 100%. Go figure.

THE DARK

I'm afraid of the dark. I used to think this was kind of embarrassing as an 'adult' but now I understand it is one of humanity's most ancient primordial fears based on something quite sensible. Don't leave the cave because you can't see well and you'll probs get eaten by a bear. As opposed to bears, I tend to imagine various monsters from horror movies I watched at an inappropriately young age that don't actually exist, but I like to think the urge to never expose my back to a dark room will one day save me.

TREES

Hear me out on this one okay. I'm not 'afraid of trees' – I'm afraid of scary trees in scary places. I think forests are generally spooky and have that whole 'what evil lurks within?' getting lost vibe, but as I referenced above, when I was nine I watched *The Blair Witch Project* on the TV in my room at 5am and it literally traumatised me. Don't do that.

SPECIFICALLY MAN-MADE OBJECTS UNDERWATER

Turns out there isn't an actual name for this. 'Thalassophobia' is the fear of the sea, but I'm fine with the sea! Man I love the sea. I've been diving, I've jumped off cliffs, I'm even one of those 'let's swim over to that island over there' kind of maniacs. No fear of abyssal depths or standing on crabs, but put me near a buoy or a boat and I will FREAK OUT. I don't know what it is but I just can't stand man-made things underwater. Ropes, anchors, ladders – you have nightmares about murderers and apocalypses? I have them about falling off an oil rig and accidentally touching a slimy pipe.

MOTHS

Don't trust 'em. Unlike graceful and composed butterflies who swoop and ascend serenely, moths can seemingly instantly dart a metre in any direction. You need to always be prepared for contact. Also as a late-night laptop-in-bed user – who invented a creature attracted to light? A cruel joke.

SPIDERS

Okay pretty basic and uninteresting but OMG SPIDERS ARE GROSS. Funnily enough I'm fine with tarantulas! I know a guy who had one as a pet and it was kinda cute. I don't really mind tiny spiders who'd get squished if you sneezed towards them, but there's a special middle ground which I just cannot stand. I feel like it might have something to do with a particular traumatic memory.

Warning – if you find spiders gross you might want to flay yourself after reading this.

SPIDER-ON-CHEST INCIDENT

I was nine. Back then I asked my parents for a bunk bed in my room, no idea why – I think I just found them exciting whenever I went to a hotel with them so the idea of being able to sleep in a top bunk at my discretion was indescribably exciting. It was a hot summer's night and I was sleeping bare-chested with the covers off and the windows open. In the middle of the night I awoke because of a strange tickling on my chest. I reached with my right arm down the wall to the light switch and I looked back to see the biggest, blackest, meatiest, hairiest house spider (Tegenaria Domestica if you want to look it up, I have no idea why you would) was descending from the ceiling directly above my face and trying to crawl up my neck. I have never flipped out quite like I flipped out at that moment. I screamed and thrashed wiping myself with the bed sheet in an attempt to scrape it off, barrel-rolled directly off the top bunk five feet onto the floor and slapped myself in the chest about fifty times. I ran out of my bedroom all the way downstairs trembling with horror when my mum ran out of her room in a panic just to laugh when I explained what happened. Thanks. I slept on the sofa for three days.

PHIL'S PHEARS

*The opportunity for a title pun was there, I had to take it.

HORSES

I don't trust their legs or intentions. Also one time I actually rode one at 'Horse World' and when I got home a load of black liquid ran out of my nose? Suspicious.

BURGLARS

I live in constant fear that someone is going to climb through my window! I think my future house will have bullet-proof guard tigers and robotic airlocks.

THE SEA

This is my main 'fear' as it were. I've always felt uneasy about deep sea water. I think part of it is just human nature as why would anyone want to plunge themselves into freezing cold salty water that is potentially filled with sharks and jellyfish and as yet undiscovered man-eating seaweed? I have had some traumatic water-related incidents though. The story I'm about to tell made my friend Louise cry-laugh so feel free to also enjoy my pain.

THE SNORKELLING INCIDENT

I was 14 years old and on a dream holiday to Australia with my parents. We were about to fulfil most people's ultimate life goal: snorkelling in the Great Barrier Reef. I realise how lucky I was, this was the thing at the top of everyone's bucket list and a once in a lifetime experience! In typical Phil fashion I had the worst day ever.

We got a large boat to the middle of the reef and before we started our snorkel adventure, the captain asked if anyone wanted a flotation device; a huge pink marshmallowy thing that wrapped around your lower half. I thought 'No! I can do this! I know how to swim,' so I declined the crotch marshmallow and jumped into the water. I then realised that many of the fully grown dads and teenagers were wrapped in lovely floating pink cocoons while I was immediately flailing around and drinking half the sea.

The idea was that we had to swim 'about a mile' to a small island and have lunch on it! I could see no island. Was this some kind of joke? I spun around in circles until I noticed a tiny dot on the horizon. That was the island. I tried to put my feet down and gather some energy until I realised the seabed was lined with razor sharp coral. 'Pull yourself together, Phil! If these tiny babies can swim in the sea so can you!' I thought, as I started doggy-paddling towards the island-shaped dot. I swam a good few metres and may have seen the flash of a fish when suddenly a small wave descended on my face and filled my snorkel with water. I flailed a lot. For some reason I thought rolling over would be a good idea which led to me filling my nose with half of the ocean and losing my mask which immediately sank to the bottom. I like to think a tiny fish is using it as a home right now.

Without a mask I couldn't see anything and all around me I could hear families saying, 'OH LOOK, TILLY! A BLUE STARFISH!' 'Mummy! Look at the conga eel!' 'The dolphin is letting me ride on its back Jonathan!'.

I wasn't going to let this beat me. I was going to make it to the island. I tried one final kick of triumph when one of my flippers slipped off and drifted into the distance. With one flipper I was now swimming in circles. I was defeated. All I could do was lie on my back and cry 'Help! Hellllp! Hellllllllllppp meeee!'.

A few minutes later a 19-year-old lifeguard that looked like he was from *Home and Away* had lifted me onto a giant lilo and was dragging this crying pale lump of failure across the sea to the island. Everyone watched as he deposited me onto the sand like a beached whale. At least I could enjoy my lunch now!

'Who wants a cheese sandwich??'

I THINK MY FLIES ARE UNDONE
I THINK MY FLIES ARE UNDONE

STOP RIGHT NOW

Do me up Dan! I mean, whisker me up

SHERLOCK IS CANCELLED

OOH ♥ JEMIMA

#Stopphil2014   CheeSE umBRella

BUY it on i-Tunes

I'D FREAK OUT IF I SAW YOU IN THE BATH

LIZARDS

THE GAME

THOSE GUMS ARE PRETTY MOIST

The year is 2087

I bought you a spaniel

im obsessed with animals...

I THINK WE SHOULD STOP !!!

I THINK WE SHOULD STOP

YOUR BUTT WON'T BE THE ONLY THING THAT GETS WIPED TONIGHT

AMERICA ATTACK

HEY YOU HAVE REALLY GREAT TEETH

Timmy likes it !!

TODAY I'M HAVING ANOTHER EXISTENTIAL (R)SIS!

i CAN'T ESCAPE THE FREEDOM!

it's been 16 years

Poo

PHIL AND DAN IN JAPAN

P: I WANT TO GO BACK!

D: Okay, Phil, you should probably rewind yourself a little bit.

P: Oops, let's try that again.

D: Hey why is your name first in this title?

P: 'Phil and Dan in Japan' just sounds way better than 'Dan and Phil in Japan'.

D: You win this round!

P: Out of every country in the entire world it had always been my biggest dream to visit Japan.

D: Me too! We're what you would call 'gigantic weeaboos' – that means people who are obsessed with anime, video games, sushi and Japanese culture in general.

P: Our favourite games are Final Fantasy, one of our favourite movies is *Kill Bill Volume 1*! The showdown at the house of blue leaves.

D: Thankfully our trip didn't involve any mass dismemberment, but yes! Going to Japan is something we've always talked about doing, so halfway through writing this very book we thought 'Hey! Why don't we randomly go to Japan right now and say it was for the book?'

P: Best plan ever. So I did something very un-Phil like and booked the tickets that very moment. No going back. We were going to Japan!

D: Well, we almost didn't make it.

P: Yeah that may have been my fault.

D: At the airport just before our flight, I asked Phil to check the departures screen who told me 'Yeah, we have loads of time!' when in reality we had five minutes before the gate closed.

P: I thought the gate would be nearby and it'd be no problem!

D: Our gate was 25 minutes and two monorails away.

P: I've never been so stressed.

D: In that situation I just like to let the inevitability of the situation wash over me and know there's nothing I can do, but Phil went into full-on panic mode.

P: I remember looking Dan directly in the eyes and saying, 'That's it. We're definitely going to miss our flight.'

D: Then he started to sprint, literally sprint to the gate.

P: I think it was more flailing.

D: He bounded through the airport like a roadrunner made of spaghetti and I followed, coughing up my lungs. OF COURSE as this was us two, our gate was on the fifth floor so our running included a fun five flights of stairs. I literally nearly died.

P: We were the very last people there, but when we arrived the gate was still open. With my dying breaths I asked the gate lady if we'd nearly missed the plane and she said, 'Oh you had loads of time! We just like to send the message early so the passengers aren't late.'

D: GEE THANKS A LOT, 'LINDA'.

P: So after the worst ten minutes of my life we got on the plane and we made it! And here is what we did in Japan:

169

AKIHABARA

D: The land of technology, anime merchandise and life-size character body pillows, it's Akihabara!

P: This was one of the places I felt the most Japanny.

D: You can't just invent words like Japanny, but I know what you mean! There were neon billboards, arcades and cosplayers everywhere.

P: Beware of venturing into the basements of anime stores though, I'm still bleaching my eyes after a certain tentacle incident.

D: Phil!

D: We were starting to get hungry after so much fanboying; so we decided to go to a Maid café!

MAID CAFÉ

P: I was actually nervous about this as I had no idea what to expect.

D: A maid café is themed around the idea that you are a Victorian lord being waited on by your maids.

P: They sing to you and make you 'magical lattes'; you can even choose what animal is drawn on your drink! I went for a lion and Dan of course went for an alpaca.

P: After our drinks we were each given a choice of a maid to have a photo with. I didn't realise we could have one with our waitress too and she looked so sad when I didn't pick her!

D: Coco is still crying right now.

P: Stop! Intimidatingly you have to go and stand on stage in front of everyone and choose some props out of the maid's box and have a Polaroid taken that she writes on for you as a souvenir! I know this sounds kind of creepy, but it was all innocent! Apparently it's quite touristy.

D: You say that but there were some 'regulars' I noticed in a corner.

P: Nothing weirder than the horde of crazy cat lady regulars we saw at that cat café in London.

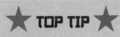

★ TOP TIP ★

We wouldn't recommend eating a main meal at a maid café as the food looked quite basic and expensive! Just go for a drink and maybe a dessert.

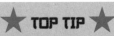

★ TOP TIP ★

There are also butler cafés! Instead of Japanese maids, in these you are served by British guys so we gave this a miss as it didn't seem very exotic to be served a cup of tea by Graham from Cardiff.

SHIBUYA

D: Shibuya! An entertainment and fashion district that is also home to the insane crossing where *checks Google* around 45,000 people cross each day.

P: I felt like I was in a stampede of orderly wildebeest.

D: I felt very much like Mufasa crossing that road.

P: Spoilers, Dan!

D: Oh come on, that movie is like 20 years old. Anyway, we decided to have some fun and make a game we're calling 'Where's Philly?'

P: Or 'Where's Phildo' if you're American!

D: ...as if I say it.

Can you see Phil in his red jacket?

P: Another landmark of Shibuya is the saddest statue in the world – Hachikō!

D: Hachikō is a dog whose owner used to meet him every day outside the train station. One day his owner died and Hachikō waited outside the station for his master every day for ten years until he died too.

P: Dan, you're making people cry.

D: This dog went on to become a national treasure and they built a statue in his honour! Here we are mourning him:

'PURIKURA'

These photo booths can be found on the top floors of most arcades! They are famous for making you look slightly alien-like as they automatically enlarge your eyes and make your legs longer to make you 'beautiful'.

You can also decorate your pictures with futuristic pens. Here's some of our terrifying creations:

HARAJUKU

P: Gwen Stefani wasn't lying as the harajuku girls do have wicked style.

D: And the boys.

P: And the crepes!

D: Oh my god the Harajuku crepes were life-destroyingly good. I am foaming at the mouth just remembering them.

P: Brb. Going back to Harajuku to buy a crepe.

D: If you've been to London, Harajuku felt a bit like Camden! It was very cool and market-like with loads of stalls, unusual stores and kooky fashion.

P: Also Dan bought so much anime merchandise from one store he got a free tissue box.

D: I'd never been so happy.

⭐ TOP TIP ⭐

If you want to visit a mall go to 'Sunshine City'! Not only does it have an aquarium with seals in the ceiling (sealsing?) but it is home to the largest Pokémon shop in the world! Warning: You may spend your life savings like we did.

MEJI JINGU

D: We couldn't spend a week in Japan without absorbing some culture!

P: So we decided to visit a shrine called Meji Jingu hidden away in the middle of a forest in the city.

D: The entrance to the shrine or 'Torii' was huge!

Apparently you are supposed to walk around the outside of it, as you can only walk through the centre if you are a god. Of course Phil walked right through unknowingly.

P: Then we arrived at a place where you write prayers on pieces of wood and hang them from a tree. Dan wished for people to be nice to Kanye. I wished for pandas to mate more frequently ... AND IT CAME TRUE.

D: It did! I remember it being in the news when we arrived home. They should call you the panda whisperer.

P: I prefer 'Panda Lord'.

SHINJUKU

D: Tokyo's organised crime/red-light district. Yay!

P: I expected it to be seedy and weird but it was actually pretty cool!

D: We went straight to the famous Robot Restaurant Show which is the most insane two hours I have ever experienced in my life. Basically a crazy/ amazing guy spent over £50,000,000 on turning a building into an insane holographic casino with a show about giant robots.

P: At one point a man in a gorilla suit rode into the room on the back of a giant robot moth and got shot by a woman in a bikini firing a bazooka.

D: If that sentence doesn't sell it to you then nothing will!

P: Here's a picture of a gigantic robot hawk that doesn't really do it justice:

D: We also visited the famous bar in the hotel from *Lost in Translation* so we could pretend to be Bill Murray!

P: AMAZING BURGER (and views)!

STUDIO GHIBLI MUSEUM

P: If you're a fan of Ghibli movies then this is a must! It's a special museum designed to give you a tour of Hayao Miyazaki's mind.

D: It was very magical. We even got to see an exclusive Ghibli movie which used human voices for each sound effect and our ticket was a film cell!

MOUNT FUJI

P: Before we begin, do you want 'Phil's Fuji Facts'?

D: I'm sure this will be fun – okay, Phil!

P: Mount Fuji is called Fuji-San in Japanese! It's an active volcano that last erupted in 1707, and a dragon nestles beneath the mountain guarding a huge pile of gold.

D: I think that's The Lonely Mountain from *The Hobbit*.

P: I ran out of interesting facts.

D: One of our favourite days in Japan was our excursion to Mount Fuji! We decided to do everything ourselves on this trip but for this adventure we needed a guided tour as it's 100 miles outside of Tokyo and we can't navigate our way to a Tesco let alone a faraway mountain.

P: As with every form of transport, we almost missed the bus!

D: Only because literally everyone in Japan needed to pee in the one toilet in the bus station.

P: It seemed like it. We ran for the bus and were greeted by our incredible host and tour guide Riko! The first thing she did was sing an improvised song about Mount Fuji, coaches and Japan which was actually strangely amazing.

D: She then told us a story to help us remember her name. 'What's her name? Oh I can't recall … recall? RIKO! Her name Riko!' What a character.

P: She didn't stop talking for the entire nine-hour trip.

D: I think she tried to sell us an apartment at one point? Anyway, we drove through the beautiful Japanese countryside to reach Mount Fuji, stopped at a vantage point to appreciate the view, only for the mountain to be totally blocked by one troll cloud:

D: That is not my name, but yes I bought some bottled 'Fuji air' which wins the award for the most pointless/hilarious souvenir ever.

P: Will you ever drink the air out of it?

D: Maybe if the world starts to end I'll have the freshest breath ever ready to go!

Like seriously OF ALL THE PLACES that cloud could be! Nature, smh.

P: Thankfully we didn't just stare at it from afar, we got to drive up it! We stopped at 'The 4th station' where hikers leave humanity behind to ascend to the peak. There was actual snow on the ground and it was absolutely freezing!

P: We descended the mountain and went on a boat ride (with fake steam pipes) to get another great view of the troll cloud:

D: There were a bunch of lads on our tour bus who decided to wear shorts and t-shirts because it was a hot day in Tokyo, they didn't enjoy this 45 minutes.

P: So many blue knees. Thankfully they had the best inventions ever – vending machines that sell warm coffee!

D: You bought two just to put them in your pockets.

P: Totally worth it. Anyway, who are you to talk, Mr Bought-a-can-of-air-from-the-gift-shop?

Then we went on a cable car ride up to the volcanic hot springs resort of Hakone!

D: Unfortunately there was no time to bathe in the hot springs which is always my favourite part of an anime.

P: Apparently everyone has to be completely naked which may have been mildly awkward. We did see some bubbling water though!

D: Yes! There were rapturous shafts of volcanic steam bursting from the ground.

D: They also sold 'black eggs' which had been boiled in the sulphurous water bubbling out of the ground.

P: Sounds healthy!

D: I feel like health and safety wasn't taken as seriously over there. Anyhoo, we were descending the mountain and about to journey back to Tokyo, when the troll cloud decided to depart and we were greeted with a perfect view of the mountain!

P: Fuji-san revealed himself! It was like looking at a perfect cartoon mountain, it was incredible!

P: I ate some black ice cream, which gave me a black mouth for the rest of the day. It just tasted of vanilla which was kinda disappointing.

D: What were you expecting?

P: I dunno! Ash? Dragon blood? At least black cherry or something.

D: It really was the perfect end to an amazing trip! We then got to travel back via bullet train which in my head was built up to be some mega futuristic space-vehicle but turned out to be like any fast train.

P: I was kind of disappointed that it didn't feel like a rollercoaster with robot butlers on board pouring you tea. Also it was where we had to say goodbye to Riko so I was emotionally vulnerable.

D: She and her strange songs will be in our hearts forever.

TOUR GUIDES

D: It wasn't just Riko we had escorting us around!

P: No thankfully, as otherwise I'm sure we would have gotten lost, walked into Godzilla's cave and been eaten, we had two fellow YouTuber friends living in Tokyo, Duncan and Mimei!

D: Having two fluent Japanese speakers allowed us to enjoy just smiling and nodding during every conversation for half the holiday.

P: Now I think about it they could have been saying anything! Like, 'Forgive our friends for being too tall and knocking everything over in your shop, British people are just damaged like that.'

D: To be honest we were too tall for most of the buildings and I would describe your clumsiness as damaging.

P: Either way I'm glad they were there. Thanks, guys!

CHERRY BLOSSOMS

D: The reason April is the most popular month for going to Japan is the cherry blossoms!

P: The super pretty trees only bloom for a couple of weeks in the whole year and depending on the weather you could totally miss it.

D: Thankfully when we descended from the sky on our journey into Tokyo, we were greeted with an ocean of pink flora!

P: It was so beautiful! I felt like I was in a slow-motion scene in a movie the whole time. Next time we will participate in the special cherry-blossom viewing picnics they call 'Hanami'.

D: They made for an ultra-kawaii very aesthetic background for photos though. We took quite a few with them.

LANGUAGE

D: Thankfully pretty much everyone we spoke to knew some English!

P: Japanese seems like the most impossible language to learn ever. Did you know there's over 50,000 Kanji (word symbols) to learn?

D: Ain't nobody got time for that! Something funny we realised was no one could understand our English due to our British accents. It sounds bad, but honestly the best way to be understood was by attempting a terrible Japanese accent.

P: Remember that time we went shopping and walked up to that thing we thought was a parade?

D: Oh you mean the one that turned out to be an anti-tourism protest? Yes. Maybe it would be good if we could read some Japanese.

FOOD

P: You better like Sushi and noodles if you visit Japan as there was a LOT of Sushi and noodles!

D: Yeah interestingly, unlike Britain, there were hardly any foreign-food restaurants, but we love Japanese food so it was like heaven for us!

P: I'm not sure about their traditional breakfast though. No offence, but I'm not really in the mood for pickled fish and miso soup first thing in the morning! Thankfully there were enough waffle and pancake places to keep me alive for the whole trip. If I had my blood tested I think I would be 18 per cent maple syrup.

D: The only thing I didn't like was the fermented soy beans.

P: I think if you put the word fermented in front of anything it's probably gross.

D: Fermented cheese.

P: Fermented bees.

D: Okay, let's stop.

SUBWAY

P: All people told us about before we left was how apparently complicated the Tokyo subway system was! Thankfully for us there was an app that just told us where to go.

D: Yeah we were fine but I think before apps existed we would have died of old age trying to navigate through the tunnels.

P: The weird thing is how gigantic the stations are! We once walked 500 metres from the entrance to one of the lines.

D: We realised that if you're travelling less than a mile you might as well just walk above ground and inhale some fresh air/sakura petals.

P: Also we were too tall as we kept being hit in the face by the handles. Japan wasn't built for people of our lengthiness.

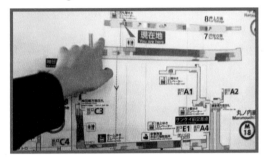

One other cool thing is that each train has its own jingle for when it arrives! More things should have jingles.

D: What like?

P: Toasters? Umbrellas? Kettles? I just need more jingles in my life.

THEMED CAFÉS

D: You think the idea of a cat café is exciting? You know nothing.

P: Tokyo is obsessed with themed cafés. These are places that serve food and drinks like any normal café, but with a crazy theme! And we mean crazy. Here's just a few we stumbled across:

Snake Café

Owl Café

Penguin Café

Ninja Café

Vampire Café

Robot Café

Final Fantasy Café

D: There was even a 'Tokyo Ghoul Café' based on an anime about cannibal monsters where all the food was made to look like human flesh! We avoided that one. Now I'm hungry.

GACHA MACHINES

P: These are machines where you insert 100 Yen and get a random prize inside a plastic egg!

D: You were obsessed with them!

P: Who doesn't want a keyring of a cat riding on the back of some sushi or a deer brandishing a hammer?

And if you were a pro like me, you could make it extreme by gambling on the 1,000 Yen machine! There were hundreds of mystery prizes ranging from new computers to jewellery, but would you risk £5 on nothing?

D: I remember how excited you were about pressing that prize button.

P: It could have been so many cool things, but no, of course I got a gold purse that's probably worth 50p.

D: Stellar use of your money there, Phil.

SAYONARA!

D: And that was our trip to Japan!

P: I almost had to buy a new suitcase because we bought so much stuff.

D: How'd it compare to England for you?

P: It's like two different worlds, I'm not sure I could live there but I absolutely loved visiting and will definitely return. I want to bring back one of their toilets.

D: Really?

P: It's hard to go back after experiencing a warm seat with butt-spray action.

D: TMI. I'd like to go back and see some more rural Japan outside of Tokyo at a different time of year!

P: See, it was totally worth going just for this book.

D: That was a good idea, wasn't it? Damn maybe we should have done it more often and gone to Disneyland.

P: Or on safari!

D: Let's not kid ourselves – you'd probably get eaten.

P: True. Well we hope you enjoyed reading about our adventures!

D: Sayonara!

P: I WANT TO GO BACK!

THE PHANGA

A DAN AND PHIL MANGA VOL. 1

ART BY ARCTOIDS

STORY BY DAN AND PHIL

TAP
TAP

FRINGE CHECK!!!

MILD BREEZE

...

WELL, HERE WE ARE, DAN-KUN, FIRST DAY BACK AT SCHOOL!

SO DID YOU FINISH ALL THE HOMEWORK OVER SUMMER?

WHO ARE YOU STARING AT?

ZACK STRYKER-SAN, CAPTAIN OF THE CEREAL CLUB!

N-NOTICE ME, CEREAL SENPAI!

MILK

ATTENTION PLEASE. SCHOOL IS CANCELLED TODAY, YOU MUST ALL RETURN HOME IMMEDIATELY.

WHY?

THERE WAS AN ACCIDENT IN THE LAB WITH THE SCHOOL MASCOT...

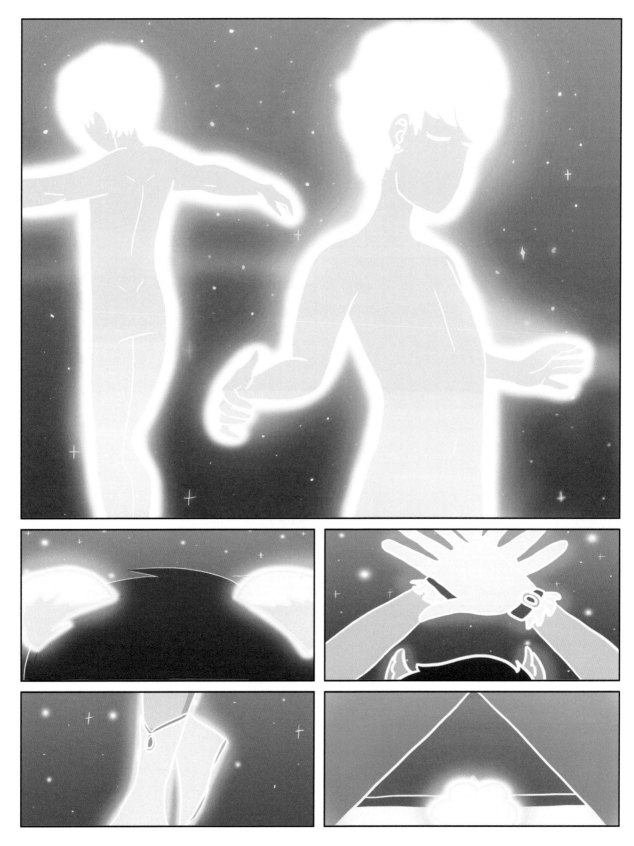

I DON'T REMEMBER THIS BEING SO TIGHT.

YOU NEED TO LAY OFF THE POPCORN.

HEY!

LION ABILITY 'SONIC ROAR!'

IT WORKED! I'LL DISTRACT IT.

ALPACABILITY 'CUTE-FACE!'

DAN-KUN, NO!

FRIENDSHIP!!

DAN AND PHIL, NOT ONLY DID YOU SAVE OUR LIVES, BUT YOU HAVE PROVIDED ENOUGH SQUID TO FEED THE SCHOOL FOR MONTHS!

C-CEREAL SENPAI?

SUGOI! PHIL, YOU ARE AMAZING!

I WOULD BE HONOURED IF YOU JOINED ME AS CO-CAPTAIN OF THE CEREAL CLUB!

...

I-I DON'T KNOW WHAT TO SAY, THANK YOU.

BUT THE WORLD KNOWS WE'RE MAGICAL BOYS NOW, WHAT DO WE DO?

I GUESS OUR LIVES WILL NEVER BE THE SAME.

-THE NEXT DAY-

THE END

PHOTOS YOU MAY NEVER HAVE SEEN!

THE 7 SECOND WRITING CHALLENGE

P: I'm sure all of you by now have heard of the most epic game in the universe, The 7 Second Challenge.

D: The rules are pretty simple, you have to do a challenge in seven seconds – but how can we put this in a book? I hear you ask.

P: The Seven Second Writing Challenge!

D: As we are now both experienced authors, we thought we'd put our typing speed and creativity to the test! We will give the other person a topic and they have just seven seconds to write something about them. No pressure!

P: You're going down Danny boy.

D: Don't call me that.

P: Okay, we'll take it in turns, you're up first! You have seven seconds to write about ...

P: **VOLCANOES**

D: they are hot I don't like falling in them that would hurt

D: **FLAMINGOS**

P: they are pink I dont trust their eyes or souls and they s

P: **ARTIFICIAL INTELLIGENCE**

D: it will destroy the world we need safeguards stop Facebook

D: **GOD**

P: god is on a cloud playing a flute he is everywhere or nowh

P: **PUBERTY**

D: the change is coming how embarrassing dont talk to me mum

D: **CHEESE**

P: cheese is gross and gives u nightmares I dont like it

P: **PENGUINS**

D: cold birds why can't they tfly so many movies why

D: **THE INTERNET**

P: web and information we like it and i n

P: **BEES**

D: they are the friends of the flowers not like evil wassps yay beed

D: **PHIL**

P: I am phil and i am cool Ilike movies and I have hair and

P: **DAN**

D: brown hair nice face alright guy i gyess cool clothes

D: **THE AMAZING BOOK IS NOT ON FIRE**

P: the books is the best book of all time I am enjoying writing

D: STOP. Well that was something.

P: Who won?!

D: I dunno, man, I think my writing on 'bees' was pretty poetic.

P: You typed 'beed' at the end.

D: Don't you mean 'u', Phil? I saw what you did for Cheese, blatant cheating.

P: More like cheese-ting.

D: So what do you think, should we use this method to whack out the rest of the book in record time?

P: I'm thinking no.

D: I whole-heartedly concur.

What Dan and Phil Text Each Other

What even is this

It looks like ⚡ got drunk

Lol 🍸

⌚⁉🔛

🎐🛡🌐

🖼🖼📍

📝📖🔖

let's stop

Ok
Delivered

Sarah Michelle Gellar just follow Friday'd me and I don't know what to do

hahahahahah

oh god

oh man

the best and worst thing

i think you have to acknowledge it

Thanks for the follow Friday @realsmg birthday made!

Something like that?

or reply to her tweet with something classy and understated like 'ah thank you! this tweet is the best birthday present i've had today 😊'

Did you take keys

Did you?

No

WHAT

We're locked out??

It's Sunday we can't get spare keys today we'll have to stay with someone

Loljk I took keys
Delivered

I hate you

---

here is some salt and pepper magnified

O0o

It looks like that Scottish rock I want to chew it

household dust..

Gross

Wtf is that anenome

idk its probably on your eyelid right now

💀

Plz get me some chocolate or something

Do u rly need chocolate

Yes u don't know what I've been through today

What sitting on your laptop for 5 hours

There were two wasps in the lounge

🐝🐝

Wow ok I'll buy chocolate
Delivered

Where are u

Having dessert at a weird restaurant with a dog

Omg I want to eat it

The dessert not the dog

Thanks i presumed that
Delivered

'should i bring a coat? nah it's not raining sky looks clear and i'm just in a taxi'

I'm going to drown walking to boots

omg

you don't need to go to boots

i think my hair will survive

I think I just deleted the sims

What

Why are you even on my pic

Pc*

I'm installing that badger game

Well how did you delete an entire program check the recycle bin

The sims is in the bin

That's just the shortcut you spork omg
Delivered

😩

What time is it?

There is literally a clock on your phone

I meant day

That is also on your phone
Delivered

Oh yh

Going Deep with Dan and Phil:

ROBOTS

D: Alright, Phil, it's your turn. Set us up!

P: Hello and good evening/morning/lunch/dinner o'clock people of the book and welcome to Going Deep with Dan and Phil. Today I, the honourable and wise Philip Lester the Third–

D: You're just the first.

P: Don't ruin my moment! Would like to start a discussion.

D: Sure, Phil, what do you want to talk about, zips? The joy of midnight cereal?

P: Please, Dan, give me some more credit. I wanna talk about ROBOTS.

D: I'm sure you're picturing some kind of giant fighting thing but I'm pretty confident I can take this somewhere interesting.

P: Dan, how do you know that I'm not a robot?

D: Really? Um, lots of reasons.

P: Give me just one!

D: You have two-hour showers, which can't be good for a robot!

P: Waterproof skin, duh. Just as I thought you can't prove that I haven't been a robot built to spy on you this whole time!

D: Okay, how's this, why would anyone program a robot to be as clumsy as you?

P: Okay, you got me there. I'm not a robot! Just in case you were still wondering.

D: Thanks for clarifying.

P: Do you think there are any super robots out there though?

D: Nah. If that kind of technology existed the Japanese would have already used it for something creepy everyone could buy. I think that the power of Artificial Intelligence will be one of our worries in the future though.

P: It's crazy how quickly things are advancing. I bet by 2020 our phones will be able to holographically tuck us into bed at night.

D: That is an incredibly disturbing thing to imagine. Everything is built for Americans anyway. I wouldn't trust something with holographic powers to understand my British accent.

P: So what's to worry about? Surely we can just program the computers to behave and be nice friendly toasters and vacuum cleaners that can whip out puns when your happiness levels are dropping?

D: Just imagine, Phil, what if the robot unprograms that safety program itself?

P: Woah.

D: It's called a 'singularity' and it's the inevitable doom we're hurtling towards. *The Matrix* was a prophecy, I'm telling you now.

P: I kind of want that meteor we were talking about in our first Going Deep to arrive now.

D: Don't worry, hopefully we'll be long dead before any such technology exists to oppress us.

P: That's a weird way to put it, Dan. I think we should just keep the robots to cute small things that couldn't possibly rebel and murder us. Like whisks and toothbrushes.

D: We already have an electric whisk and toothbrush.

P: See! The future is now! Let's stop advancing things before we regret it.

D: Do you think if we ever get smart enough to program emotions that computers will have souls?

P: Dan, that's too deep. Too deep for Going Deep.

D: But seriously! Do you think you would date a computer program? I don't think I could. You would always know you are basically dating the descendant of a microwave.

P: Plus I think humans have a certain spark of humanity that makes us do things a robot never could! Like today when you were out, I was practising my wolf howl. I don't think a robot could handle that randomness.

D: Yeah if a robot tried to understand your brain it would probably fizzle out or explode.

P: If you could have any kind of robot what would it be?

D: Probably some robo-shoes that would make me exercise.

P: I'd make the ultimate robo-chef! It would make all my meals and wake me up with a funnel of coffee carefully placed in my mouth.

D: You'd just be one of those guys from *Wall-E* with no need to move or go outside ever again.

P: I think I would miss trees actually. I do love a good tree.

D: That's good to know, Phil.

P: Though in the house of the future I bet I could have holographic tree wallpaper with an HD camera streaming from deep within the rainforest.

D: You'd finally be at home, at one with the monkeys.

P: I feel like we've bonded during these two Going Deep chats! I'm going to miss it. Can I come into your room at 4am for deep and meaningful conversations?

D: Remind me to buy a lock for my door.

P: Or get your robot butler to do it.

D: Bzzzt.

P: BBBzzzzt. Oops I spilled Fanta on our circuit boards.

D: Error

PHIL'S AESTHETIC

THE DAN AND PHIL ALBUM

Left to right
Right to left
Everybody's whisking up and down
Back and forth
Up and down
Everybody's whisking Delia Smith's face

S-s-s-s-s-s-s-s-s-s-s-s-sieving yeah
Sieving Sieving
It gets the ████
Work those arms
That'll give you the right muscles
To do the thang

Egg egg egg
It's the king of all yolks

It's a breakfast bar stool
It's a breakfast bar stool

It's Japanese witchcraft
How do they do it I don't know
It's this and this it's this but how

It's a purple mushroom
It's a cola thing
It's a horrible teacake
Yeah yeah yeah

Fork of justice
Sailing through the night

Can you please get murdered on
a different road I'm trying to film

Spicy spice
Spicy spice
Spice the spice and the spicy spice
Cajun spices spice in the pan
Spicy fajitas yeah man

It was the night before Christmas
And all through the sea
Jellyfish were stinging your
entire family

It's the crime dance
It's the crime dance
Yeah
Crime

I like bananas I like bananas in the sunshine
Sunshine sunshine bananas
I like bananas I like bananas on the moon
Moon moon moon

Milk quest
It's the best
Milk in your face
Not cows

Rave time rave time rave time
Rave time rave time rave time
Don't step on the glass
Don't step on the glass
Tinsel in your foot
Bauble in your foot
Bauble in your eye

Everybody cries when you go to
A&E with a bauble in your face
Blood
Blood everywhere

Hyper kirby plumber and sword

Beat the butter and the sugar till its done
Beat the butter and the sugar till it's done
There are ghosts inside your butter
There's a skeleton in the sugar
And it's really spooky today
on Halloween

Shake shake the sugar
It's what 'ya cane gave 'ya

Susan you only had a short life
But now you're on the bar
And everyone is sad
Susan

Lizards they're my favourite spikey reptile
So scaley
Lizards I'd freak out if I saw you in the bath
Cold blooded
Lizards

I wanna pour it all over my naked body
Except I don't as I'd burn to death

Spooning the milky wheat onto the darker base
Yeah

Dripping all over his body
It's dripping dripping yeah
Making a tattoo as I'm dampening your neck

Let's buy a stool
Let's buy a stool
But first we need to go to the kitchen
Go to the kitchen
Then it will be an option
This is the kitchen song

Slenderman Slenderman
Does whatever a slender can
Can he jump from behind
Yes he can

Space space
I stick it in ya face
But there's no air
Where? Space
What

Harajuku Harajuku
You might find a pikachu under the bench
There is no stench because it's amazing
In Japan

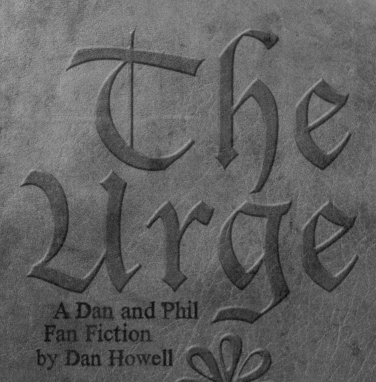

The Urge

A Dan and Phil
Fan Fiction
by Dan Howell

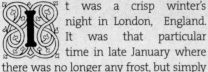

It was a crisp winter's night in London, England. It was that particular time in late January where there was no longer any frost, but simply biting cold air in what felt like a completely empty atmosphere.

Dan Howell was walking down the road; his tall black silhouette cast shadows from the artificial amber glow of streetlamps. His breath formed swirls of mist with every exhalation and he decided to slide his exposed hands inside his coat pockets to retain some warmth. The street was empty at this time and his footsteps echoed up and down around him, only interrupted by the cruising hum of a taxi driving past. He wasn't totally alone after all. Dan had time to think on this journey, time to think about what had happened the night before.

The events had played in his head so many times over that he didn't know whether he could trust their accuracy, or if his own perceptions had rewritten how the events unfolded. Any way he thought about it, one thing was certain. His friend, Phil Lester, was dead.

Phil had a habit of always being in the worst place at the worst time. It was an endearing quality that often resulted in funny stories for him to share with his friends or his followers on the internet. He was a kind person. Perhaps that's why he was singled out as a victim. It wasn't fair. A painful stab of recollection shot through Dan's brain, as if forcing itself through a wall he had built to protect himself. He saw it again. The dead, lifeless eyes, the way it moved so swiftly out of the darkness, the blood. The blood was the most vivid memory of all. Dan had somehow found himself collapsed in a corner, unable to move, but out of the corner of his eye he saw the crimson trail

of his friend's life weaving around the cobbled stones of the street and down a drain. Dan saw his hand twitching, those last moments of resistance and hope that something, someone, would be able to save him. Then it stopped. That is the last time he saw Phil Lester alive.

Dan arrived home at their apartment. It felt wrong. Opening the door to the living room, the usual bright colours of their possessions seemed inappropriate, disrespectful even. How could anything dare to be so bright at this time? He turned off the lights and collapsed on the grey carpet of their hallway. Sleep.

The next day was to be Phil's funeral. Dan had no interest in going. His friendship with Phil was personal to him and not something he wanted to share with family and friends who would mean well but insult with every word of comfort. He decided that even if he had to attend physically, he would be somewhere else in his mind. He had to.

Dan remained silent and stoic through the service. People left to return to their lives, the relatives trading condolences, leaving Dan alone in the room with the coffin. He didn't want to look – it would be real if he saw. He wanted to run away as fast as he could from this nightmare, but he had to see. Dan strode over and gazed into the box. Lifeless. Even with Phil's typically pale skin you used to see the warm glow of life within. All that could be seen here was the sickly pale-green colour of death.

Dan went to turn away, to walk out of the room into a life where everything familiar was gone, when something grabbed his wrist.

'Don't go, it's okay.' Dan turned to see the same pale skin he had just had burned into his memory gripping at his shirt.

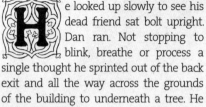He looked up slowly to see his dead friend sat bolt upright. Dan ran. Not stopping to blink, breathe or process a single thought he sprinted out of the back exit and all the way across the grounds of the building to underneath a tree. He vomited. It wasn't real. He was hysterical. He tried to rationalise the thoughts in his head as his eyes shook with distress.

'Dan, stop running, I'm not going to hurt you.'

He spun around to see Phil, standing upright as if completely fine with his hands forwards as if anticipating Dan's irrational behaviour. 'You can't, I mean, this can't be real,' Dan said, grasping behind his back to try and hold onto the tree as if it was a tether to reality.

'You know I'm real, Dan, this is real and I think you know why.' 'No!' Dan shouted and pushed Phil backwards in utter disbelief. Phil grabbed Dan's wrists and pinned him against the tree. Dan could feel the sharper edges prodding uncomfortably into his back as if the tree itself was pushing him towards the nightmare. 'It was a vampire.' The words penetrated into Dan's head and seemed to pull down on his soul as if everything he had been trying not to believe in the last two days was sinking like quicksand. 'I don't know how, or if that's exactly what it is, but it explains it well enough,' Phil said in a calmer tone, clearly aware of Dan's slow realisation.

'You aren't the real Phil,' Dan said in a flat, emotionless tone. His head was bowed and in Phil's grip it seemed Dan wasn't trying to resist anymore. 'If what you're saying is true, you aren't Phil. You're just a beast possessing his body.' He looked up and stared into Phil's eyes. He didn't see the bright blue pools of life that he used to, he saw emptiness. He must be right.

Phil stared back at Dan, seeing his brown irises blazing with fury. Phil let his grip loosen for a second. Dan realised and swung a punch as hard as he could, hitting Phil square in the jaw. Phil reached towards his lip. Blood. He looked down at it in a strange way and glanced back up at Dan who seemed to almost be expecting something. Phil decided to wipe the blood on his shirt. 'I won't lie,' Phil said, rearranging his suit jacket and sweeping his black hair away from his eyes. 'I feel different. I feel urges. I still know who I am, what I do, what the difference is between right and wrong. And yet something is within me, something primal ...', 'Shut up,' Dan said, clenching his fist and visibly shaking with rage. 'You are not my friend and if I have to destroy his body to give him peace, do not think I won't.'

Dan spun around, reaching for the sharp wood that was cutting into his back. In one sure motion he snapped the branch and immediately swung towards Phil, who, as if in slow motion, leant backwards, smacked the branch from Dan's hand and grabbed him by the throat. Dan's head banged against the tree with a force that shook the leaves from the branches, falling over the boy's shoulders. His breath was heavy. He could feel the beads of sweat forming on his forehead. This was fear. He tried to move but the force his friend was applying to his neck seemed immovable and impossible.

Phil stepped closer until their noses touched and looked Dan directly in the eyes: 'I could kill you. Every fibre of my being is urging me to tilt your head back and bite your neck, but I can choose not to.'

'What?!' Dan said, spitting out warmth before taking in a huge gasp.

'I don't want to kill you. I want you to join me.'

Dan felt his heart drop in pressure. An overwhelming stillness waved through his body until he was stunned into silence. 'No p-please,' he stuttered.

'You don't have a choice, but I do. Appreciate it,' said Phil. 'Think about it, Dan, things can continue like normal! We can tell everyone it was one of those miracle situations where I was never actually dead. We can go back to our apartment and continue our normal lives ... with some dietary adjustments, I guess.'

Dan had completely lost his ability to think. Part of it made sense, maybe it would be okay if he didn't have to lose his friend, or his own life. He knew it wasn't true though. Even though Phil was right in front of him, there was no breath coming out of his lips. The only sensation he experienced was the damp chill of Phil's skin pressing against his.

Just then Dan noticed a man who must be the groundskeeper walking by in the distance. Dan had made his choice, and he knew it would be the right one. 'HELP!' Dan shouted, shaking as hard as he could, causing Phil to almost loosen his grip. 'He's trying to ki–'

Then he felt it. Two sharp stabs pierced the skin of his neck. Dan dropped his arms and buckled his knees, he had lost.

Phil moved in closer, pinning Dan's body against the tree as he gulped gallons of thick blood through his teeth and down his throat. Phil almost felt himself losing control, feeling a desire to completely give in to a more powerful force within himself. 'No,' he said, pulling away, feeling the blood run down his neck past the collar of his shirt. Quickly he raised his wrist and pierced his own veins. 'Drink!' he ordered, pressing his wrist against Dan's mouth. Dan, with the last moments of his fading energy attempted to resist, pitifully shrugging his shoulders. It wouldn't be enough. His natural instinct to breathe opened his lips and the pungent taste of iron filled his mouth and flowed across his tongue. Dan's vision faded to black.

Blinking. Vision hazy and unclear. A yellow light. A white ceiling. After what seemed like a dreamy eternity unable to move, Dan's eyes focused and noticed the familiar patterns of his bedroom ceiling. He was home. Had it all been a bad dream? Dan asked himself this as he reached to touch his bare chest with his fingers. He could still feel. Surely that meant he was still alive? His hand stopped. Palm lying flat over his chest, he tried to focus all senses on detecting something, anything. No pulse.

He looked to the right to suddenly notice Phil, sitting in a chair leaning over the bed.

'How do you feel?' he asked, with what seemed like a degree of confidence.

Dan's eyes darted up and down trying to decide what he made of this person, or whatever it was, sitting next to him. He sat up and swung his legs over the bed. Lifting his head up with a strange, new assuredness he had never felt before, he locked eyes with this friend. 'Hungry,' Dan said, feeling within him an urge, a biological mission he now felt he had to begin.

'Me too,' Phil said with a smirk. 'Why don't we go find someone to eat?'

The Hand

DAN AND PHIL FAN FICTION
BY PHIL LESTER

Phil woke up covered in sweat and screaming. He wiped his muscular brow as he got out of bed. That nightmare had been something else. 'Weird,' he said as he did his morning routine of 300 sit-ups. Dan was already in the kitchen making a delicious breakfast of bacon pancakes with extra maple syrup. 'Oh hey, D-Slice', said Phil, backflipping into the room and hi-fiving his friend in mid-air. Dan looked horrified.

'What's wrong?' Phil asked, as a bead of sweat dripped from his forehead and bounced off the mutant finger protruding out of his body.

'Your body?! There's something happening to you!' said Dan.

Phil looked down in horror to see a human hand was starting to grow out of his chest, just below the nipple.

It wasn't just growing, it was moving. In shock, Dan dropped his syrupy spatula onto his leather jeans and ruined them forever. No more leather jeans for Dan.

'We need to call the army,' he told his raven-haired friend.

'Dan, no! They'll experiment on me! I don't want to die,' Phil said, as he let out a single tear, not being afraid to show emotion in front of his true best friend.

They decided to keep it a secret.

Over the next few weeks the hand grew and grew. Phil continued to make YouTube videos, he just wouldn't film below the nipple. He had to keep this a secret from everyone.

Dan and Phil even taught the hand some of their secret best friend handshakes. It was responding to the fun. When they watched *Game of Thrones*, the hand even started twitching with glee. Later that month, something unexpected happened. Dan and Phil were finishing another pancake session when the hand started violently vibrating. 'DAN! HELP!' Phil screamed as the hand started gesticulating wildly.

Dan could only stand and watch as the hand started to extend out of Phil's chest. The hand was reaching for Dan. Instinctively he started pulling it and something happened that none of the British boys would ever expect.

After a few pulls there wasn't just a hand, there was an arm and an elbow. An entire human was being dragged out of the inside of Phil – he was giving birth.

There was a giant wet explosion. All that was left of Phil was a lump of skin and there, standing in the kitchen, was a completely naked Harry Styles.

Dan gave him a pepper pot to cover his modesty. 'Thanks for pulling me out of there, mate!' said Harry as he grabbed a pancake from the pan and walked out of the door.

Dan looked into the middle distance. His face was no longer filled with confusion. It was no longer filled with horror. It was filled with REVENGE.

To be continued.

BEAUTIFUL ART OUR AUDIENCE HAS MADE

WE HAVE SOME OF THE FUNNIEST, MOST CREATIVE AND TALENTED FOLLOWERS OF ANYONE ON THE INTERNET! IT'D BE IMPOSSIBLE TO SHOW ALL OF OUR FAVOURITE PIECES OF ART WE'VE SEEN MADE OF US, BUT HERE ARE JUST A FEW OF OUR FAVOURITES.

HORRIFYING ART OUR AUDIENCE HAS MADE

ALONG WITH THE BEAUTIFUL AND AWE-INSPIRING ART WE ALSO RECEIVE A LOT OF ART WHICH SPANS THE SPECTRUM OF HILARIOUS, DISTURBING OR BOTH! WE DELVED INTO SOME DEEP CORNERS OF THE INTERNET TO FIND SOME OF THESE. UH, ENJOY?

THE EXISTENTIAL CRISIS HALLWAY

WHY DO WE EXIST?

WHAT IS EXISTENCE?

WHAT IS THE POINT OF ANYTHING?

WHY?

DOES MY LIFE REALLY MATTER OUTSIDE OF MYSELF?

DEATH IS INEVITABLE.

WE ARE ALL ALONE.

THE PRIVILEGE OF FREEDOM IS OVERWHELMING.

IGNORANCE IS BLISS.

CONSCIOUSNESS IS MERELY A BIOLOGICAL PROCESS.

TIME EXTENDS BEFORE AND AFTER MY LIFE.

PURPOSES ARE DISTRACTIONS AND VICE VERSA.

WHAT'S FOR LUNCH?

INFINITY IS INCOMPREHENSIBLE.

HELP.

THINGS OVERHEARD WHILE WRITING THE BOOK

While trapped in our apartment writing this book, we've had many strange conversations and heard many strange things said by the other person too early in the morning or late at night. Eventually we thought we should start writing them down! Here they are.

D: I just realised my left sock is slightly damp but don't know why.

P: I want my coffin to be lined with that paper. It feels so good!

D: I just realised I'm reading this story with David Tennant's voice.

P: Is there a tiny beetle on my nose or is it just a phantom itch?

D: Do you reckon we could get an industrial-sized fan for the photoshoot?

P: I had a dream the book had popcorn-scented paper.

D: I hate that photo I look like Shrek got set on fire and hit by a truck.

P: I think we should have a page about things that we said whilst writing the book and feature what I'm saying now on that page. Pageception?

D: I just typed unicorn instead of university. Dan's Unicorn Life'.

P: How many people do you think will read this sentence on the toilet?

D: What shade of black should I use for this background?

P: Do you see loads of tiny neon triangles when you close your eyes?

D: Look there's a tiny man on the kettle!

P: Are you ever tempted to shake a small amount of salt into your hand and lick it?

D: What's 3+7?

P: I forgot my mum's name for a second.

D: Was it dogs that have clean spit? Or was that a myth?

P: I kind of want a baby just to see what it looks like.

D: I've been staring at this screen for too long, are my eyes bleeding?

P: If I ate my own tongue would it taste of the last thing I ate?

D: Why didn't you tell me you bought a motion-detecting air freshener? I just had a heart attack.

P: Do you think my shorts are too short? Combined with the frilly bits I mean.

D: Last night I dreamed that I deleted the entire book off the computer. Wait have we saved the document since we started?

PATIENT 132-54/A

Why hello the internets!

Is that what I used to say? I don't remember anymore. I would check but I'm currently having my eyes replaced with newer models so I am typing this using my psychic keyboard.

I'm sending this message down a time compression machine! Handy thing that. Apple has provided a lot of useful technology for the world over the years. Worth signing the Universal Submission Declaration if you ask me.

If you're wondering what the world is like now, mostly the same. The ultra-continent of China 2 is a fantastic place to live after the great assimilation. The news keeps talking about the ant population on Australia – that island where we keep our nuclear power and prisons. Something about multiplying and mutating, I don't believe it personally.

I remember having a great time writing the book. I obviously have it digitally saved to my iBrain drive, but I do still have a physical copy in my pod. I use it as my emotional tether in case I go too deep playing the Virtual-station and start to forget about the real universe. That was a fantastic weekend I spent with Lara Croft.

Who would have known that this would be the best-selling book of all time? Of course Phil didn't realise that he was leaning on the 0 key for so long when he placed that Amazon order. Phil has been living with that debt his whole life, poor guy.

I hope all the readers enjoy the book and it brings them happiness! All the happiness you had counted before the emotion-purge of 2025. I suppose things are less dramatic now.

Anyway I am off! I have an appointment with the dentist. Of all the things that have been innovated on in our society I can't believe you still need to get fillings, oh well.

Here's a Sexual Endingcard Dance dedicated to you!

Dan

Oh hello reader.

Wow it's been a while since I've used a computer. They feel so old fashioned! It's making me nostalgic for when I was a strapping young lad with floppy black hair. Who'd have thought that would be the standard hairstyle for elderly people now?

I'm currently sat in my energy tank on the long journey through space to colonise New Earth. The great ant war was brutal but also made me realise how much I valued my home planet! It makes me sad I'll never drink a proton milkshake or ride a gravity coaster again but I have those experiences in my mind. Literally. They are embedded into the video chip in my brain.

It's nice that YouTube still exists! I've just been watching Lord Pewdiepie who now has 400 billion subscribers across the universe. 5D gaming looks fun. It's a shame I can't play due to having half my leg eaten by the queen ant in the final battle. Who'd have thought she could use a flamethrower whilst giving birth to thousands of mutant babies? Enough about the ant war. Now is not the time for those memories.

I am over 100 years old, my body is starting to give up on me. Thankfully I'm having my head implanted onto a robotic body. I've paid a little bit extra for a popcorn machine in my chest. I'm gonna be the most popular elderly robot in the galaxy.

Thanks for reading this! Hopefully we've perfected the technology to beam my message back to 2015 and print it into the book. Writing it was one of the best experiences of my life! I can't believe the Queen actually secretly kept a copy in her toilet for all those years after her regeneration.

I have to go back into hypersleep now!

Farewell, Phil

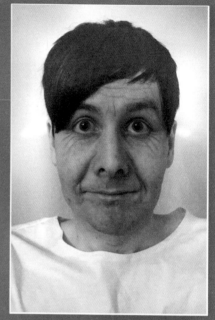

PATIENT 132-54/B

WHAT HAPPENED IN VEGAS

D: In June 2012, we went to Las Vegas. I'd never been before and we were already flying to the USA to go to the California YouTube convention VidCon, so we thought we would go a few days earlier and stop off in Nevada.

P: I love Vegas! I went once with my family when I was a teenager and it was awesome. Crazy casinos, crazy nightlife, crazy people. The only downside was I couldn't really do anything because I was too young. I actually got kicked out of The Tropicana hotel for trying to play blackjack. Oops.

D: So we decided to spend a week in the desert. Now the thing is, I kind of told everyone that I filmed the whole trip – which I did! From the plane journey there, to checking out of the hotel when we left, I had the whole thing on camera with the intention of editing it into a fun video. The story goes, when I got back to England I put it off for so long because I had filmed so much. In fact I had procrastinated so long that we lost the camera and most of the memory cards with the footage. This video-that-never-was became known as the infamous 'Vegas Video'. Everyone wanted to know what really happened with Dan and Phil in Vegas. Why would we film it all and not show everyone? Was the footage really lost? There have been more conspiracy theories than days passed since we returned from that journey.

P: We thought if those files are never to be found, then why not finally, once and for all, reveal the story in our book. So. This, is what happened in Vegas. The whole, uncensored truth.

22 JUNE 2012

P: Being 6ft tall, long flights for us aren't so much a 'ugh planes are boring and uncomfortable' as an 'omg my-legs-don't-physically-fit-in-this-seat' dangerous compression.

D: We took to the skies and enjoyed an uneventful flight over the Atlantic. This peace, it turned out, would not last.

P: We landed in the USA! I could smell the freedom the moment I stepped off the plane.

D: A short cab ride and we were on the strip. It was just as cool as it looks in the movies. I mean, it's tacky and horrible and everything about it is really seedy and evil looking, but in a cool 'Wow, I'm in a movie!' kind of way!

P: We arrived at our hotel, Caesar's Palace, and unpacked our bags ready for adventure.

D: We didn't want to waste any time, so got changed straight away and headed downstairs to the casino!

P: I'm obsessed with slot machines.

D: Phil has what you would call a 'gambling problem'.

P: It's not a problem! I'm just addicted to the bright lights and loud noises and slim chances of shiny things coming out of a hole. Okay, maybe a slight issue, but it paid off!

D: Phil, don't deny anything I have photo evidence.

P: We settled on one particular slot machine, the 'Aladdin', mainly because it had cool music.

D: And a freaking vibrating chair. Seriously the production values on these slot machines were crazy, they were basically simulators!

P: This one was special though, as you could actually win better prizes by playing little mini games, which as giant nerds who spend our lives gaming, we were pretty good at.

D: Oh man, I remember it now. We kept winning, and winning, getting jackpot after jackpot and it kept adding up!

P: We were doing so well that we started to attract a crowd of silent lurkers who usually spent their whole days endlessly pulling on the slots.

D: ... what you would have become had we stayed there any longer.

P: Hey! We weren't there for much longer though as the luckiest thing in my entire life happened, we won the mega jackpot.

D: $666,085.25 to be precise.

P: Lights went off, music started playing, the previously silent slot-lurkers started cheering with wide eyes.

D: The casino handed us a receipt we could cash in for the money whenever we wanted, but we thought hey, if we're in Vegas we need to do this properly!

P: DOUBLE OR NOTHING.

D: That's right, people. We went to play Roulette.

P: Now you may think us foolish, but we had everything going for us! Beginner's luck, the magic of youth, I was wearing my lucky socks and underpants.

D: Guaranteed win.

P: We sat round the table and watched eagerly as the ball of fate spun around the circle of fate to decide our fate ...

D: ...Okay, Phil, I think they appreciate the drama. And you will never believe this ... we won again!

P: Now you'd think this is where the story gets crazy in a good way: we cash in the cheque, rent the penthouse suite, call some of the numbers on those weird cards we got handed on the way into the casino and party all night!

D: Unfortunately not. This is when it all went horribly wrong.

P: We turned around to see two giant men in suits and sunglasses and proceeded to get dragged out of our chairs across the floor.

D: I was terrified! I had my bag and camera snatched out of my hands ...

... and they took us into some kind of interrogation room.

P: Now I've seen enough movies to know how the old 'good cop/bad cop' game is played, they didn't do that.

D: No it was just bad cop and really, really angry bad cop who wouldn't listen to us talk.

P: Basically, we were accused of cheating on the Aladdin machine!

D: I knew we were skilled gamers, Phil, but I never thought we were so good it was dangerous.

P: They kept us chained to the table all night which I thought was pretty unprofessional, then in the morning they told us some guy named 'Killer Tony' was going to have 'a tough conversation' with us unless we explained how we did it! I was so confused.

D: Oh my god, Phil, they were the mafia, they were threatening to kill us.

P: Wow that explains so much! I thought they just had it in for us because of our unorthodox sense of style.

D: To be fair our hair was pretty weird in 2012, it was probably a crime in a lot of places. Anyway, I wasn't letting this happen. You can take away my casino winnings, you can take away my freedom and it's not like I had any pride to protect really ... but you can't take my video camera!

P: Dan was really fighting for this video, guys!

D: So in a moment that I feel like all of my video game playing and thriller-watching and those two months of Taekwondo lessons my mum paid for before I quit ...

P: ... I didn't know you did Taekwondo? That's the martial art that Buffy uses!

D: I know, man, that's totally what inspired me! We're digressing. I reached under the table with my hands cuffed and with all my might flipped it over, knocking the two guys off their chairs, grabbed my camera and we ran for it.

P: We ran through the casino looking for a way out. Well, I did. Dan was too busy filming the whole thing.

D: I needed to capture our escape in case we needed it for evidence!

P: We found a staircase and ran up to the roof where we hid in the bushes from security. Again, Dan filming them probably didn't help.

D: Look at the quality evidence though.

P: We got changed into some different clothes Dan had in his bag and I began to think of a plan. Dan had his moment of braveness flipping that table like no one had ever table-flipped before, now it was my turn.

D: Honestly for someone who can't drive a car, I'm so surprised you did this.

P: I decided to steal a helicopter.

D: Now I think about it, stealing their boss's helicopter probably only made the mafia angrier.

P: Well it was his fault for leaving it on. Seriously who leaves their helicopters unlocked in this day and age? We ran up to the helipad, jumped in, I pulled up the joystick (is it called that?) and with the sun rising ahead of us, we began gunning for the Nevada desert with the mafia in pursuit.

D: We flew over what seemed like endless sand for hours, seriously America is so big though, what do they need so much land for?, when we spotted somewhere we could hide.

We didn't know what exactly it was, some kind of underground building with a lot of plain cars parked outside, but we figured whoever was there could protect us from the rampaging casino-Avengers.

P: I'm not going to lie, the landing could have been smoother.

D: Phil literally dropped the helicopter onto the roof of someone's car and we had to jump out of the window before we got chopped into slices of phan-sashimi.

P: Hey, I got us there!

D: That you did, and as our pursuers began to (safely) descend from the skies themselves we ran towards the weird building.

P: Except when we got to it, there was no entrance, just a mysterious door and a security camera.

D: I thought it was suspicious from the start if you ask me. Now we're not ones to condone vandalism, but when you're being chased by particularly broad men in suits and sunglasses, you're willing to commit some property damage in order to live. We kicked in an air-vent and slid ourselves inside.

P: You know those moments in movies where someone slides down a cave hole or vent for ages and it looks really fun? It's actually just really scary and painful.

D: Seriously. Plus it was well sandy and dusty, it totally ruined my new shorts.

P: Thank god you packed those extra clothes or we'd have looked bad on top of everything else happening.

D: Just because you get into a situation like this doesn't mean you should stop trying to look nice for people.

P: This is when our crazy story gets EVEN CRAZIER. We pick ourselves up off the floor, get out our phones to use as a torch and saw an entire underground hangar filled with incubation tanks.

D: We couldn't see through the murky glass, but something was clearly inside all of these tubes filled with bubbling liquid. There were all kinds of strange metal instruments lying around that looked unlike anything medical or industrial I'd ever seen.

P: We had to know more about this weird place, so we skimmed around the room looking for a window, which was impossible now as the sun had set, but when we looked through we saw something we'd never forget.

D: A giant machine in the shape of a triangle was hovering above the ground firing a beam of light towards the desert.

P: I started to freak out a bit so I stumbled over and fell against the wall, which is when I accidentally leaned on the automatic door.

D: 'PHWOOMPF' it slid open and we both collapsed into what appeared to be an operation theatre filled with surgeons.

P: We didn't get a good look at whatever they were operating on before some other guys in suits appeared out of nowhere and knocked us out. I go my whole life without getting into any trouble then I get arrested twice in one day, can you believe it!

D: I remember they stuck us in a lift (translation for transatlantics – 'elevator') that took us back up to a room and locked us inside. When they woke us up in the morning (no breakfast btw they were terrible hosts) they told us that apparently we were trespassing on secret government property and the well-dressed men who escorted us upstairs were from the FBI. Of course we were.

P: Dan, do you realise what this means?

D: What?

P: We accidentally broke into Area 51.

D: Oh my god, you're right. Jesus, that's typical Dan and Phil. Go for a little holiday before a YouTube convention and wind up trapped between aliens and the mafia.

P: Thankfully, this is when we got lucky in a non-money-related way!

D: Well, kind of lucky if you forget the general violence that was about to ensue. We gandered out of the window to get some sense of where we were when guess who was waiting for us, our old friends from the casino.

P: Seriously did they have no lives, who do you try to find for an entire night?

D: Thieves stealing millions of dollars from your business?

P: Okay, kind of understandable. We looked out of the window, made awkward eye contact with them, and it all kicked off. Out of nowhere they started shooting at us through the glass – like shooting someone is a good way to make them explain how they cheated on a slot machine – and we dived under the table.

D: Our well-dressed friends from the whatever-the-hell that was downstairs burst into the room to see what the hubbub was only to find themselves being indiscriminately blasted with bullets too.

P: Both parties opened fire on each other, which is kind of cool if you think about it 'Mafia vs. FBI', I wish I could have watched it!

D: They seemingly forgot about the two dorks under the table though, so we used the opportunity to dash for the nearest door when, just as we stepped outside, a stray bullet hit a gas tank on the side of the building causing a gigantic explosion! We were sent flying into a pile of rocks with our ears ringing and leg hairs lightly barbecued.

P: We picked ourselves up, glanced over our shoulders at the destruction and decided to run over the nearest hill into endless desert where we walked for hours. I was seriously hungry by this point. You don't want to mess with a Phil that hasn't had his morning cereal! It was a cool environment though so I took this pic of Dan:

D: Hey that is a cool pic! Remember to tag me in that on Facebook later, okay?

P: Sure thing. This is when I recalled a little nugget of wisdom from my grandad! 'Phil, you have no sense of direction, so promise me if you ever get lost just walk towards a road and stand on it.'

D: That's a very specific piece of advice there.

P: What can I say? He knew me well. And it worked!

D: That it did. After getting totally blanked by at least three truckers and a school bus ...

P: ...it was probably our haircuts that scared them away.

D: You could be right. A camper-van pulled over and swung open its doors. As it happened, it was some gymnasts from the Cirque Du Soleil heading back to Las Vegas to perform a show at our hotel!

P: What are the chances of that?! Unfortunately it wasn't that simple, as their offering of help came at a price. They wanted Dan and I to fill in for a colleague that broke every bone in his body practising for a trick.

D: I can say with confidence that I never once thought getting trapeze lessons would be a useful skill, but here we were. We had no choice!

P: It was either that or be abducted and probed/arrested/left with 'Killer Tony', so we said yes and hopped in the van.
Note: Generally don't hop in strangers' vans unless you are at risk of those three things.

D: They were some pretty chill dudes actually! I always wondered what it would be like to run away and join the circus. Turns out it's years of demanding exercise and really cramped cars with faulty aircon. Not really my thing.

P: The car journey wasn't our toughest challenge of the day. We made it back to Vegas, but before we could relax, it was show time.

D: The theatre was packed with about 5,000 people who all paid to see world-class gymnasts at the peak of fitness perform at their maximum. I got kind of exhausted walking up the stairs to the stage.

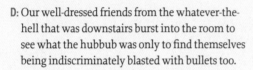
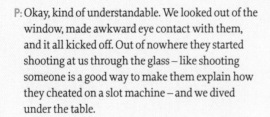

D: Phil, he clearly said 'video footage'; nothing about dozens of screenshots of that video footage.

P: If you say so.

D: We spent the night tidying the room so we didn't get an additional fine and packed our bags ready to fly to L.A. for VidCon.

P: Our new friend Francoise told us it'd be easy, we just had to stand on a diving board and hold his hands, then he'd release us and we'd fly 50ft through a burning hoop and into a swimming pool.

D: I didn't trust him.

P: Oh just because he was blocking your cool air flow in the mini-van.

D: If it wasn't for them we'd probably still have been lost in the desert, so we got up on that stage, climbed a really tall ladder and waited for our time to come when Francoise would throw us to our doom.

P: It was amazing. We jumped off and swung from his masculine frame through the air like swans as he gently released us, cascading through the air into the embrace of the water below.

D: That's a pretty poetic way of saying 'chucked us off a ledge into a freezing pond in our clothes', Phil.

P: It was one of the highlights of my life. After the show they brought us backstage, gave us a standing ovation and made us honorary members of the circus! Francoise, Janine and Ringo the sad monkey will be in my heart forever.

D: Exhausted, sandy and drenched, we crawled up to our hotel room expecting to finally rest, only to be greeted by our handsome friends from the FBI.

P: In short, they totally trashed our hotel room and told us we had to give all of the money back to the casino and that if we ever posted the video footage online there'd be 'unnecessary consequences'. Wait, isn't this what we are doing now? Dan, I don't want our book to get us hunted by the FBI.

At least I stole a couple souvenir dice from the casino to get back at them!

P: Dan, are you seriously saying after all of that you took something from the gift shop on the way out?

D: Okay, maybe that wasn't a good idea.

P: I'm just glad to finally have this story out in the open!

D: Yep! It may seem unbelievable, but that's why we never uploaded a video and this was the story of what happened in Vegas.

D: So here we are.

P: The end of our book! What do we want to say? Dan, you always like big waffly conclusions. Take it away!

D: I guess I just want to say, this thing that we've created – this world of Dan and Phil – is ephemeral. It was never something that tangibly existed, just hundreds of pictures and videos and stories and memories floating in the digital void of the internet.

It was all an accident really. We could have never met! I could have never taken that final leap into making videos, Phil might have gone back to working at a bookstore in York and none of this might have ever existed. It did happen though. We met, we made these videos together, and for whatever reason the chemistry between us had the X-factor that resonated with people around the world. And what we all created together over the following years is pretty darn wonderful. I look into that digital void and see millions of people who all found entertainment, happiness and even friendship just through these silly videos that we uploaded to a website and it makes me feel like I've really done something. I have scratched at least a tiny mark in an infinitely small part of the universe.

This book is us taking our favourite parts from that swirling universe on the internet and trapping it in something physical. Something we can hold and touch and keep in our houses, so that long into the future we can all look back and remember who these Dan and Phil guys were and what they did. You never know what might happen in the future, so in a way you could say we made this for us, for posterity, but really it was for you. Without our audience none of this would exist. I know for a fact that we have one of the most passionate followings of anyone on the internet and we appreciate it with every moment. We gave you the videos, but without the support, creativity and energy you have given us since the beginning, 'Dan and Phil'

could never have been the world that we are celebrating with this book.

The real dedication, then, is to you. You do with this book what you will. You hold whatever space for Dan and Phil in your mind that you want. We hope we represent good times in your life and that this book can be your portal back to them whenever you wish!

We are Dan and Phil, and this is The Amazing Book is Not On Fire.

P: Well how am I supposed to follow that?!

D: What? You asked for a waffly conclusion.

P: Yeah but you can't just wrap up the entire universe in an inspirational speech then walk off stage leaving me in the spotlight.

D: Say whatever comes to mind!

P: Okay, well double everything Dan said from me! Also I just wanted to say that I've really enjoyed making this book and I'm so excited to see what the future of this crazy adventure of my life will hold. Thank you!

D: How do we end it then? Self-destruct? A giant photo of a cat?

P: Maybe a derpy photo of us?

D: Sounds like a plan.

P: Thanks for reading. You are all better than toast.

Dan and Phil: Goodbye!

Goodbye!